# THE SUIT™

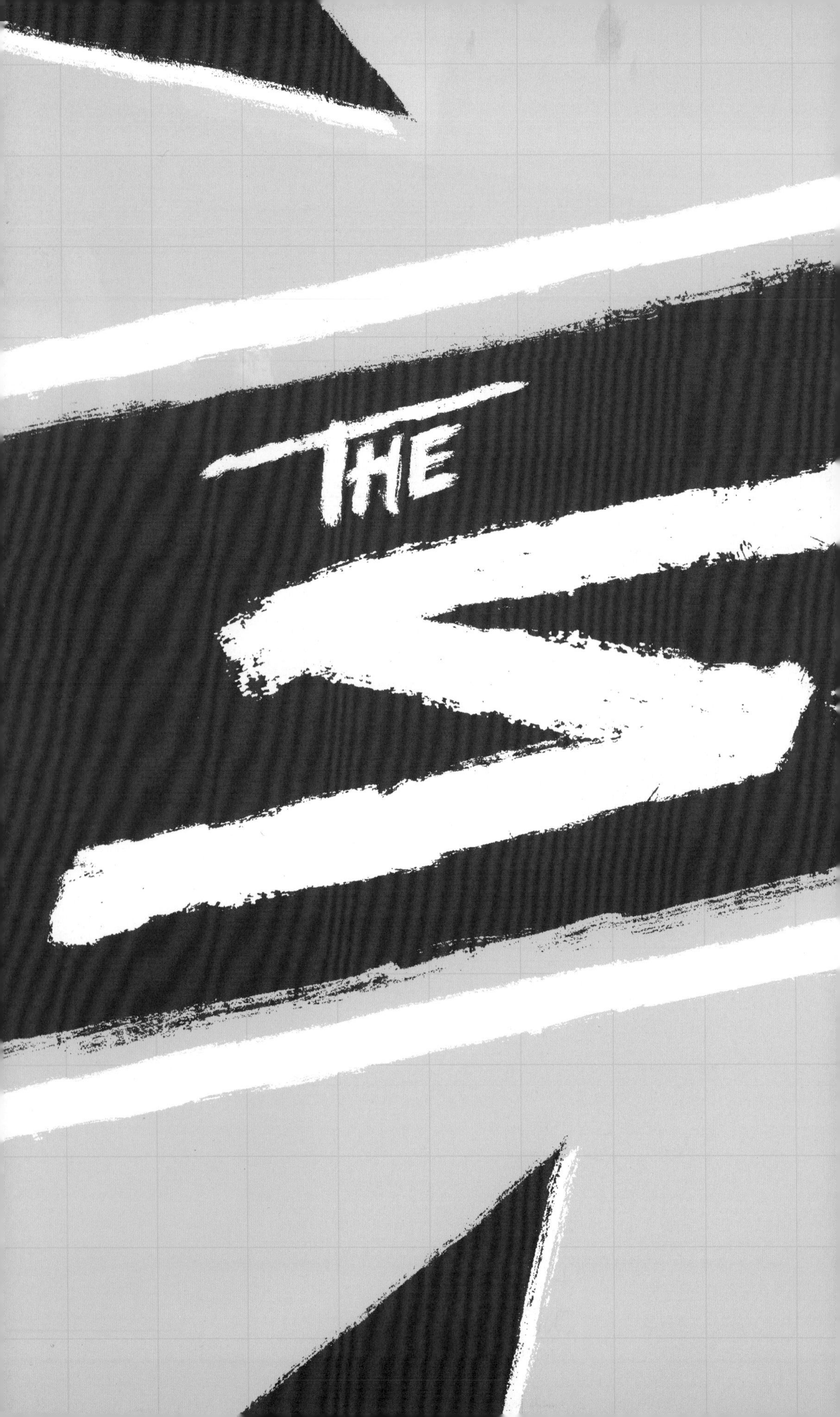
THE

WRITTEN AND ILLUSTRATED BY

## DENNIS CALERO

LETTERED BY

## JOHN J. HILL

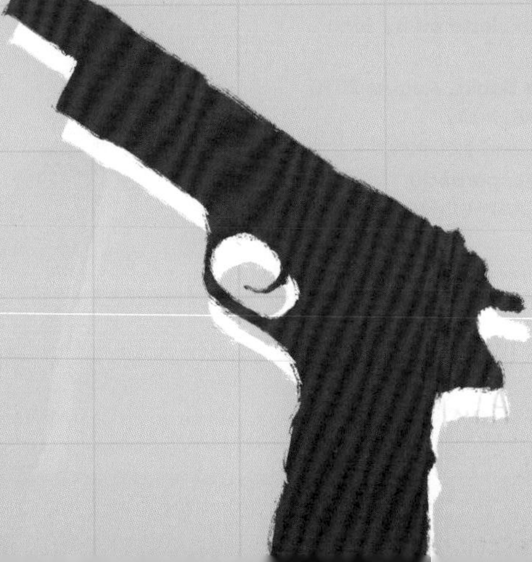

DARK HORSE BOOKS

PRESIDENT AND PUBLISHER
**MIKE RICHARDSON**

COLLECTION EDITOR
**MEGAN WALKER**

DIGITAL ART TECHNICIAN
**ADAM PRUETT**

DESIGNER
**SARAH TERRY**

ORIGINAL SERIES EDITORS
**JIM GIBBONS** AND **RACHEL ROBERTS**

SPECIAL THANKS TO RACHEL ROBERTS

*THE SUIT*

This volume collects all nine chapters of *The Suit*, originally serialized in *Dark Horse Presents* 3 #10–#12, #16–#18, and #21–#23.

Published by Dark Horse Books
A division of Dark Horse Comics, Inc.
10956 SE Main Street, Milwaukie, OR 97222

DarkHorse.com

To find a comics shop in your area, please visit comicshoplocator.com

First Edition: August 2018 | ISBN 978-1-50670-632-0
Digital ISBN 978-1-50670-633-7

10 9 8 7 6 5 4 3 2 1
Printed in China

Library of Congress Cataloging-in-Publication Data

Names: Calero, Dennis, writer, illustrator. | Hill, John J. (Letterer), letterer.
Title: The suit / written and illustrated by Dennis Caler... J. Hill.
Description: First edition. | Milwaukie, OR : Dark Horse... | "This volume collects all nine chapters of The Suit, c... serialized in Dark Horse Presents 3 #10-#12, #16-#18...
Identifiers: LCCN 2018017870 | ISBN 9781506706320
Subjects: LCSH: Graphic novels. | BISAC: COMICS & G... Mystery. | COMICS & GRAPHIC NOVELS / General.
Classification: LCC PN6727.C26 S85 2018 | DDC 741.5...
LC record available at https://lccn.loc.gov/2018017870

# INTRODUCTION

If you're
holding this volume in
a book store or a local comic shop, just buy
it. You'll love it, trust me! I'll wait.

Okay, I assume my ruse has worked and you're sitting in your study with a fine dry martini (and over 21) about to delve into the strange world of *The Suit*.

I never really know what to say when I talk about my work. Like most writers, I'm sure, I just get ideas and I want to make them. There was something interesting to me about a James Bond-type character, an operative, who didn't work for King and Country, but rather for a Reagan-era corporation.

Being set in the eighties—which seems to be all the rage these days—I couldn't help making some allusions to eighties culture. But I promise the references to a certain businessman turned politician was planned and executed, if not printed, before said individual won the big chair. Such is life sometimes.

We're fascinated by the general idea of putting on a well-tailored suit, the ultimate symbol of civilized man, and committing murder and mayhem. Well, I am, anyway. I wanted to take the sleek, cool brutality of *Le Samouraï*, and other neo-noir European films (and the Americans who were influenced by them, like Michael Mann), inject some cheekiness, and see what happened.

If that sounds weird, it is. So, I'm grateful to Mike Richardson, Jim Gibbons, Rachel Roberts, and Megan Walker for the chance to make this off-kilter story.

And I want to thank you for buying it, because that's what you did. You're not standing in your local shop still debating whether or not to buy this book.

Because I might have to send someone to convince you.

And you wouldn't want that.

Trust me.

—DENNIS CALERO
APRIL 2018

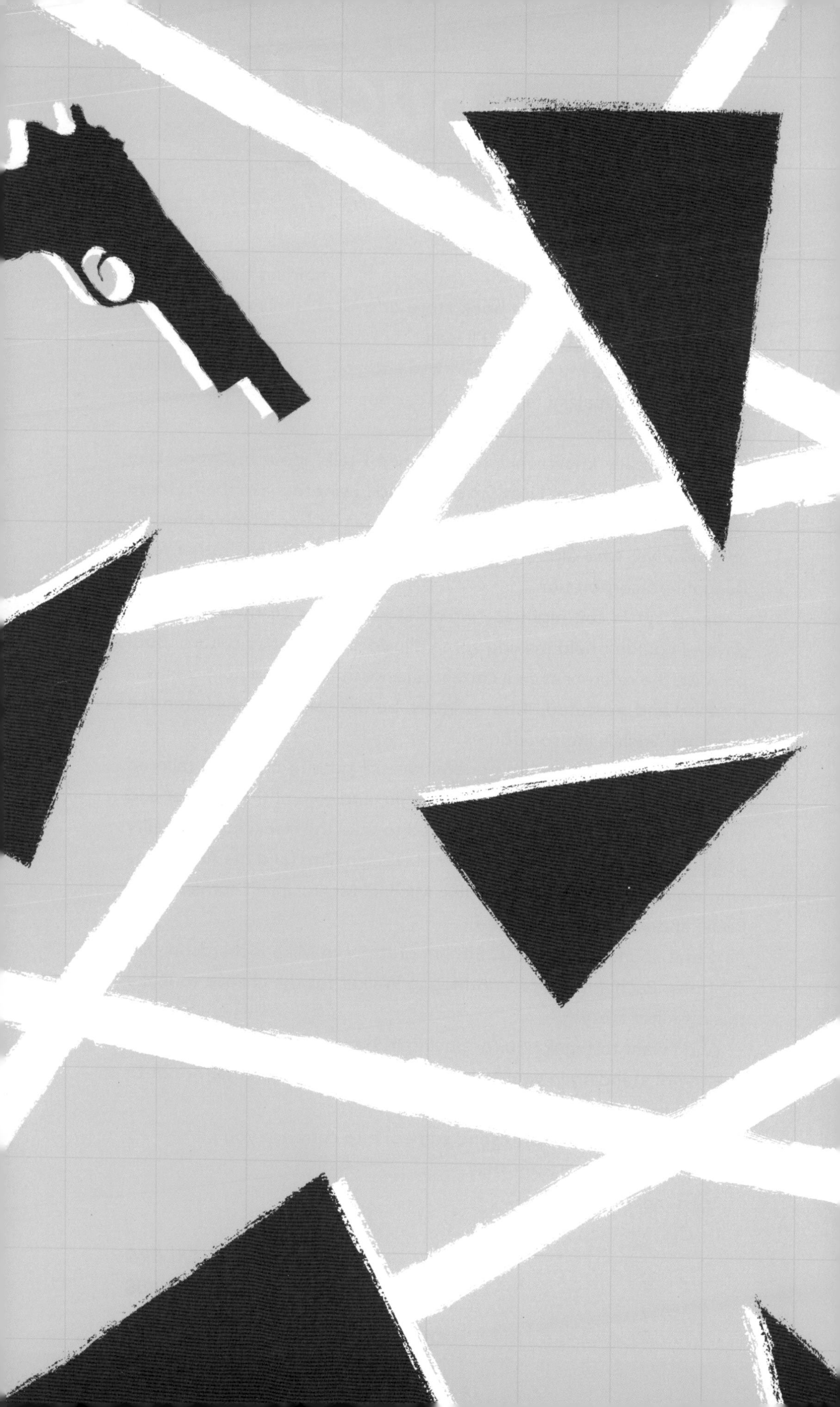

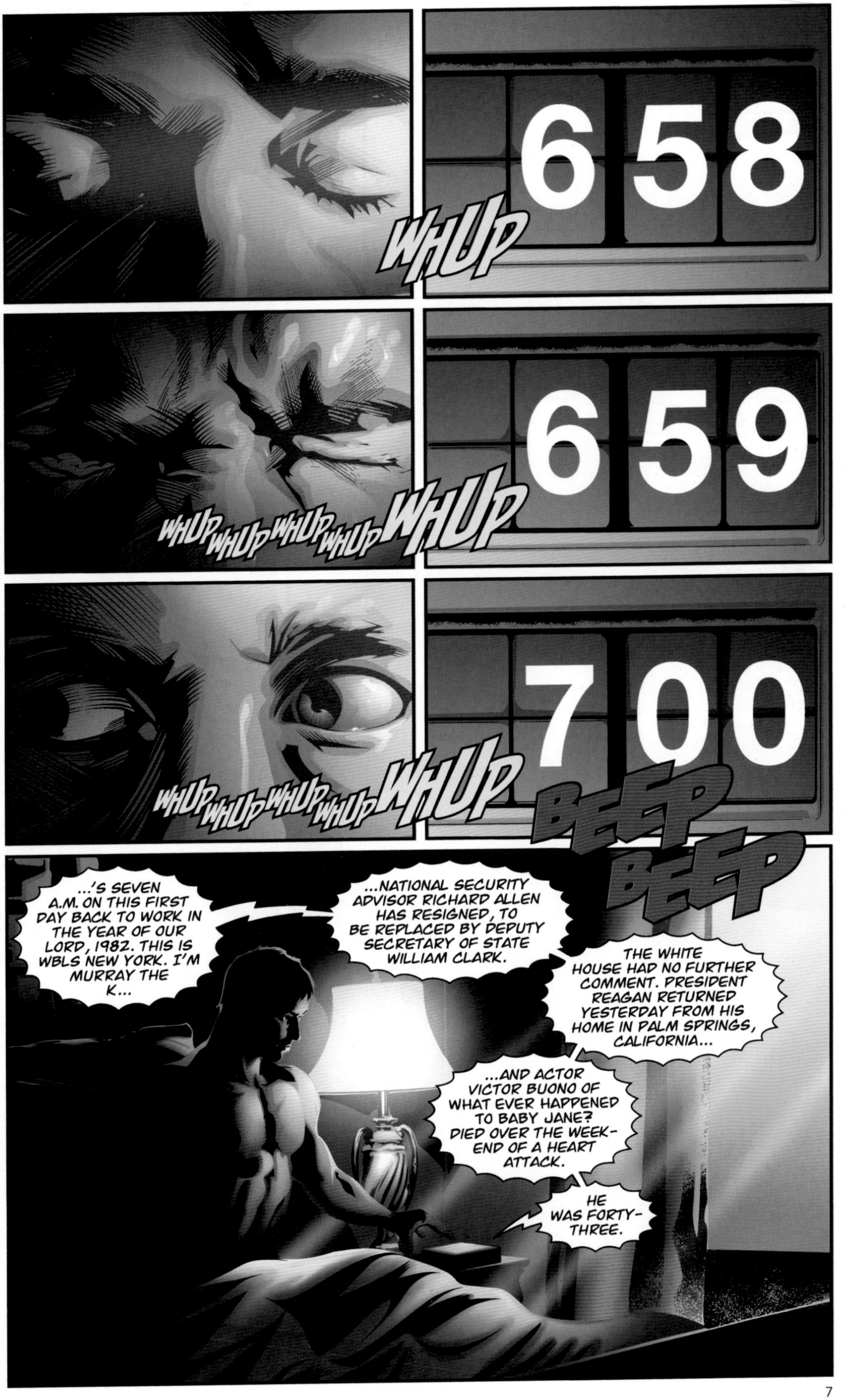

658
WHUP
659
WHUP WHUP WHUP WHUP WHUP
700
WHUP WHUP WHUP WHUP WHUP
BEEP BEEP
...'S SEVEN A.M. ON THIS FIRST DAY BACK TO WORK IN THE YEAR OF OUR LORD, 1982. THIS IS WBLS NEW YORK. I'M MURRAY THE K...
...NATIONAL SECURITY ADVISOR RICHARD ALLEN HAS RESIGNED, TO BE REPLACED BY DEPUTY SECRETARY OF STATE WILLIAM CLARK.
THE WHITE HOUSE HAD NO FURTHER COMMENT. PRESIDENT REAGAN RETURNED YESTERDAY FROM HIS HOME IN PALM SPRINGS, CALIFORNIA...
...AND ACTOR VICTOR BUONO OF WHAT EVER HAPPENED TO BABY JANE? DIED OVER THE WEEK-END OF A HEART ATTACK.
HE WAS FORTY-THREE.

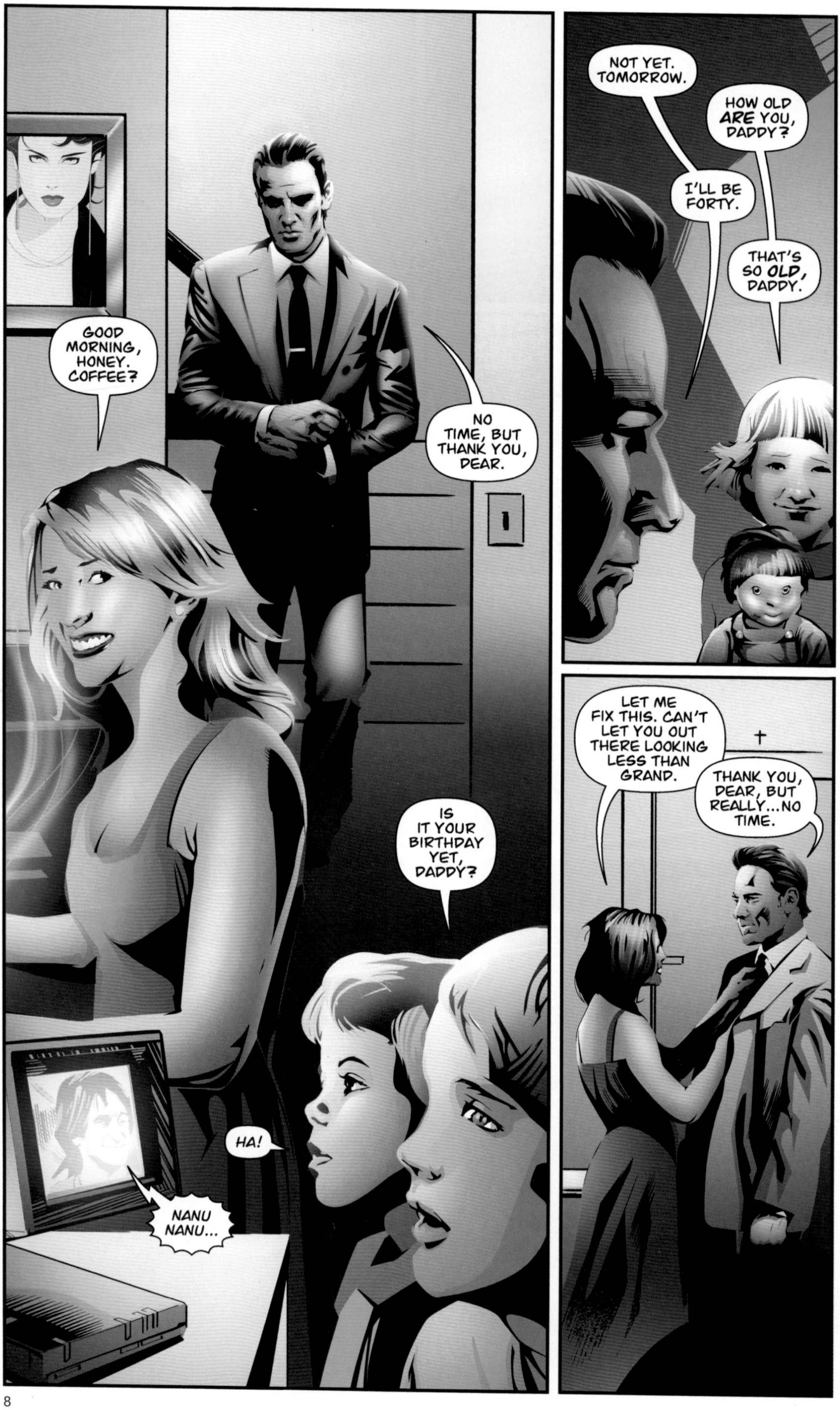
GOOD MORNING, HONEY. COFFEE?
NO TIME, BUT THANK YOU, DEAR.
IS IT YOUR BIRTHDAY YET, DADDY?
HA!
NANU NANU...
NOT YET. TOMORROW.
HOW OLD ARE YOU, DADDY?
I'LL BE FORTY.
THAT'S SO OLD, DADDY.
LET ME FIX THIS. CAN'T LET YOU OUT THERE LOOKING LESS THAN GRAND.
THANK YOU, DEAR, BUT REALLY...NO TIME.

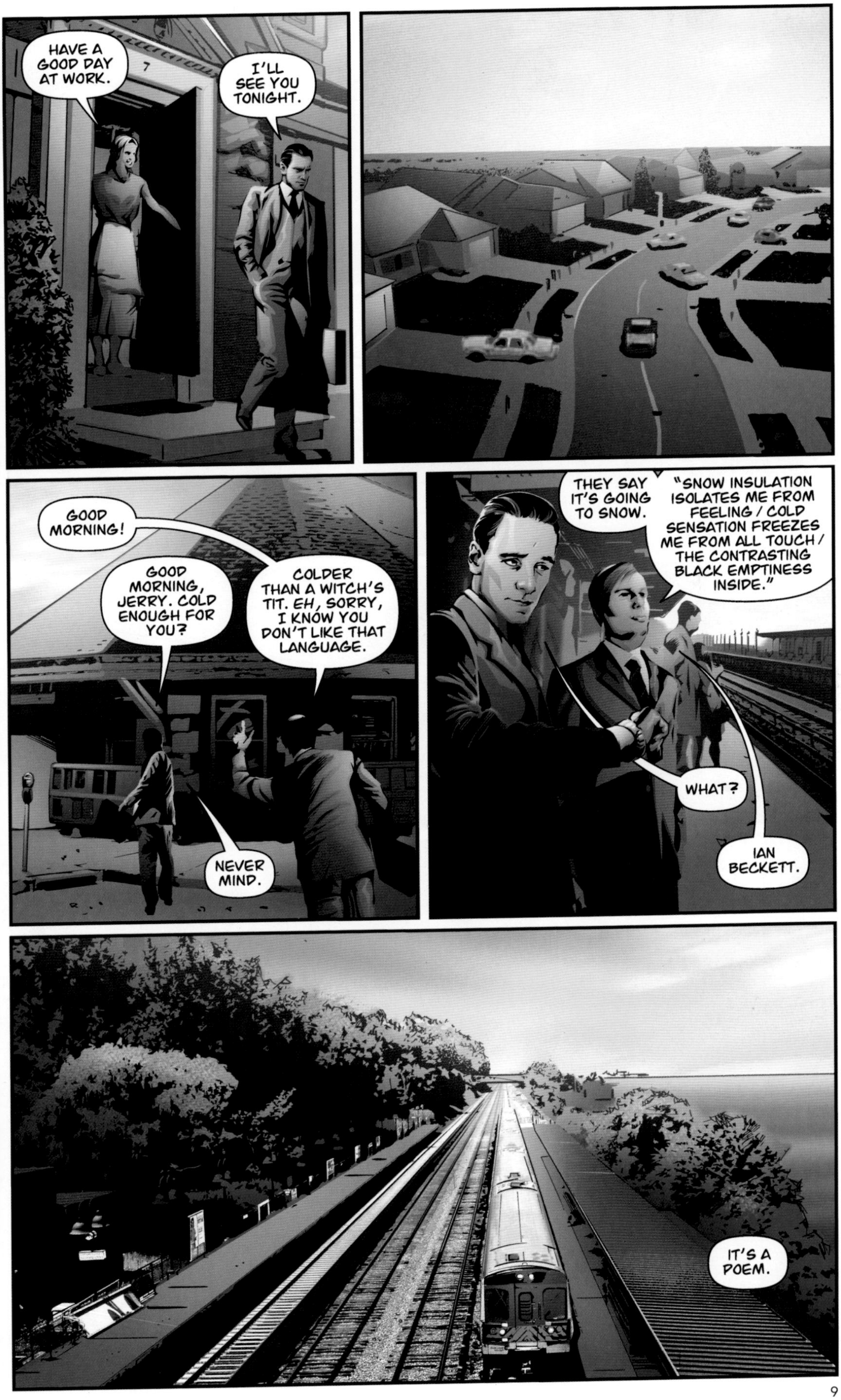
HAVE A GOOD DAY AT WORK.
I'LL SEE YOU TONIGHT.
GOOD MORNING!
GOOD MORNING, JERRY. COLD ENOUGH FOR YOU?
COLDER THAN A WITCH'S TIT. EH, SORRY, I KNOW YOU DON'T LIKE THAT LANGUAGE.
NEVER MIND.
THEY SAY IT'S GOING TO SNOW.
"SNOW INSULATION ISOLATES ME FROM FEELING / COLD SENSATION FREEZES ME FROM ALL TOUCH / THE CONTRASTING BLACK EMPTINESS INSIDE."
WHAT?
IAN BECKETT.
IT'S A POEM.

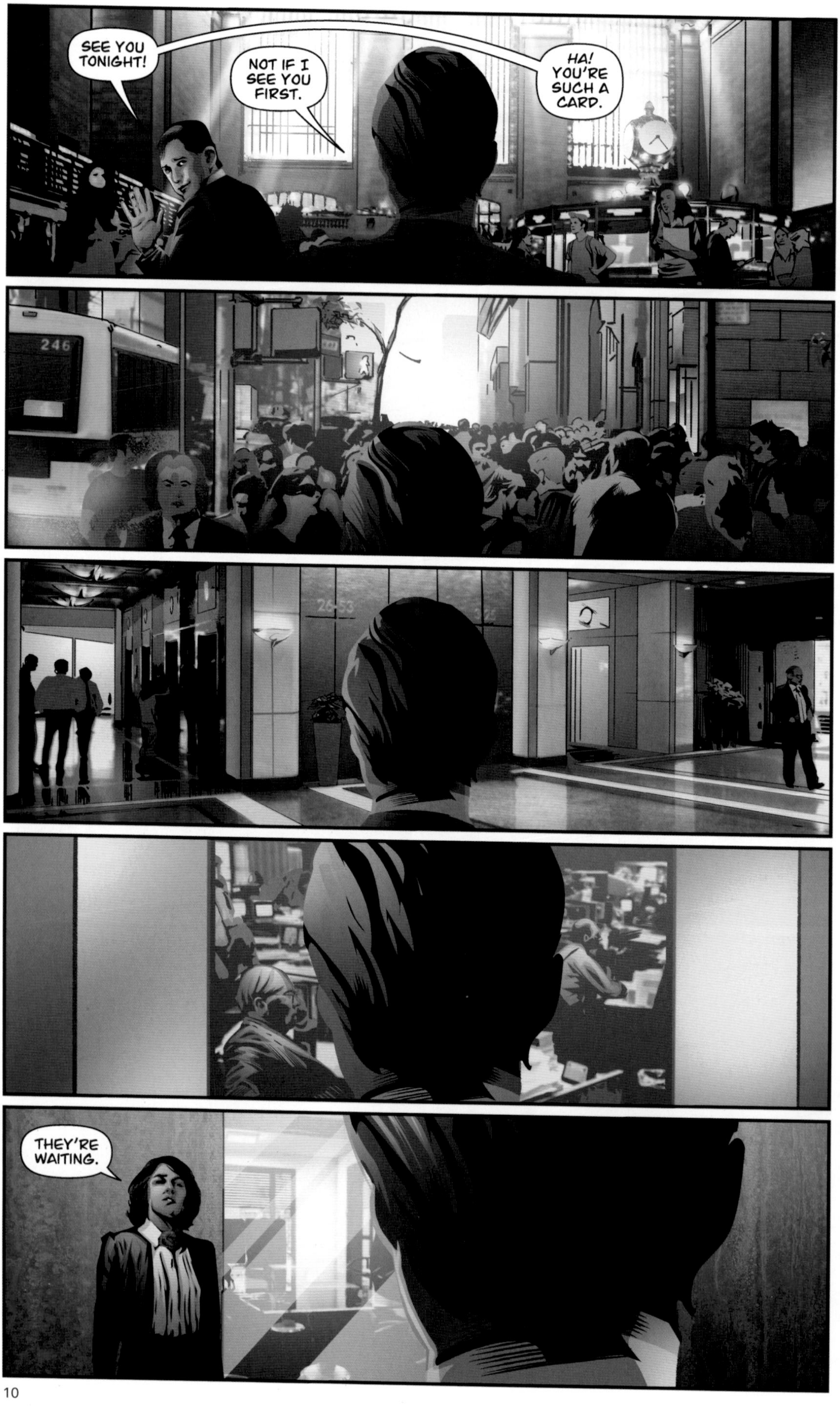
SEE YOU TONIGHT!
NOT IF I SEE YOU FIRST.
HA! YOU'RE SUCH A CARD.
246
THEY'RE WAITING.

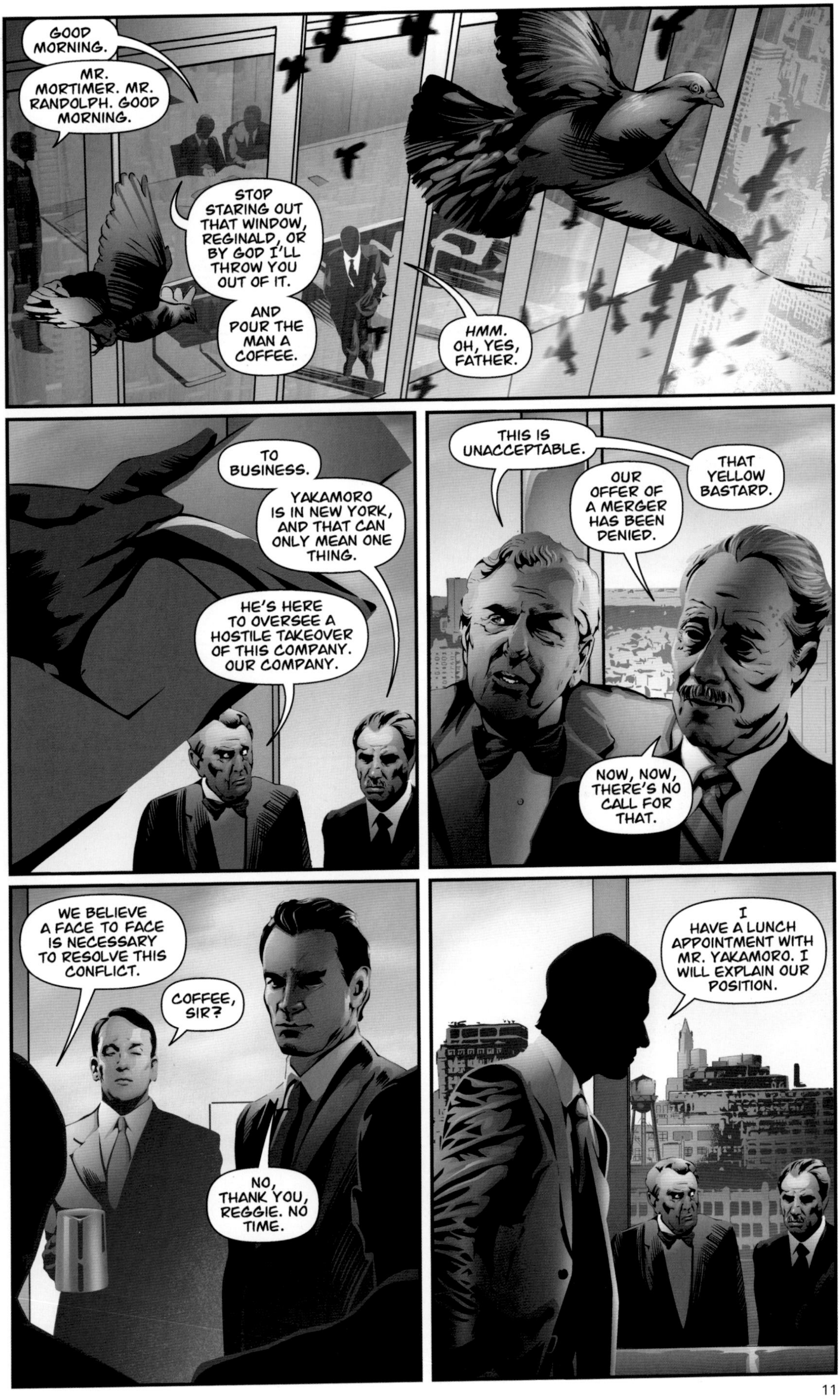
GOOD MORNING.
MR. MORTIMER. MR. RANDOLPH. GOOD MORNING.
STOP STARING OUT THAT WINDOW, REGINALD, OR BY GOD I'LL THROW YOU OUT OF IT.
AND POUR THE MAN A COFFEE.
HMM. OH, YES, FATHER.
TO BUSINESS.
YAKAMORO IS IN NEW YORK, AND THAT CAN ONLY MEAN ONE THING.
HE'S HERE TO OVERSEE A HOSTILE TAKEOVER OF THIS COMPANY. OUR COMPANY.
THIS IS UNACCEPTABLE.
OUR OFFER OF A MERGER HAS BEEN DENIED.
THAT YELLOW BASTARD.
NOW, NOW, THERE'S NO CALL FOR THAT.
WE BELIEVE A FACE TO FACE IS NECESSARY TO RESOLVE THIS CONFLICT.
COFFEE, SIR?
NO, THANK YOU, REGGIE. NO TIME.
I HAVE A LUNCH APPOINTMENT WITH MR. YAKAMORO. I WILL EXPLAIN OUR POSITION.

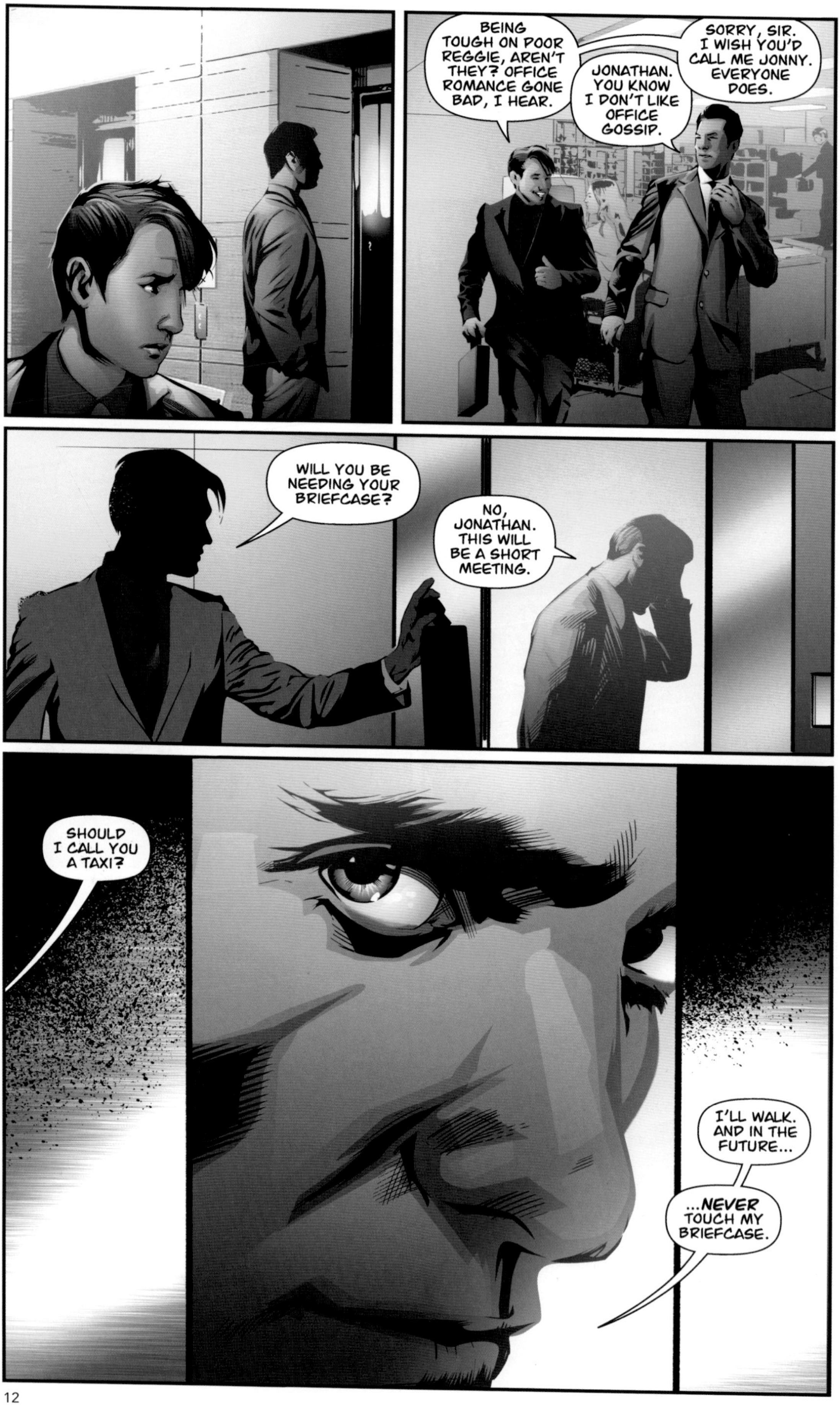
BEING TOUGH ON POOR REGGIE, AREN'T THEY? OFFICE ROMANCE GONE BAD, I HEAR.
JONATHAN. YOU KNOW I DON'T LIKE OFFICE GOSSIP.
SORRY, SIR. I WISH YOU'D CALL ME JONNY. EVERYONE DOES.
WILL YOU BE NEEDING YOUR BRIEFCASE?
NO, JONATHAN. THIS WILL BE A SHORT MEETING.
SHOULD I CALL YOU A TAXI?
I'LL WALK. AND IN THE FUTURE...
...NEVER TOUCH MY BRIEFCASE.

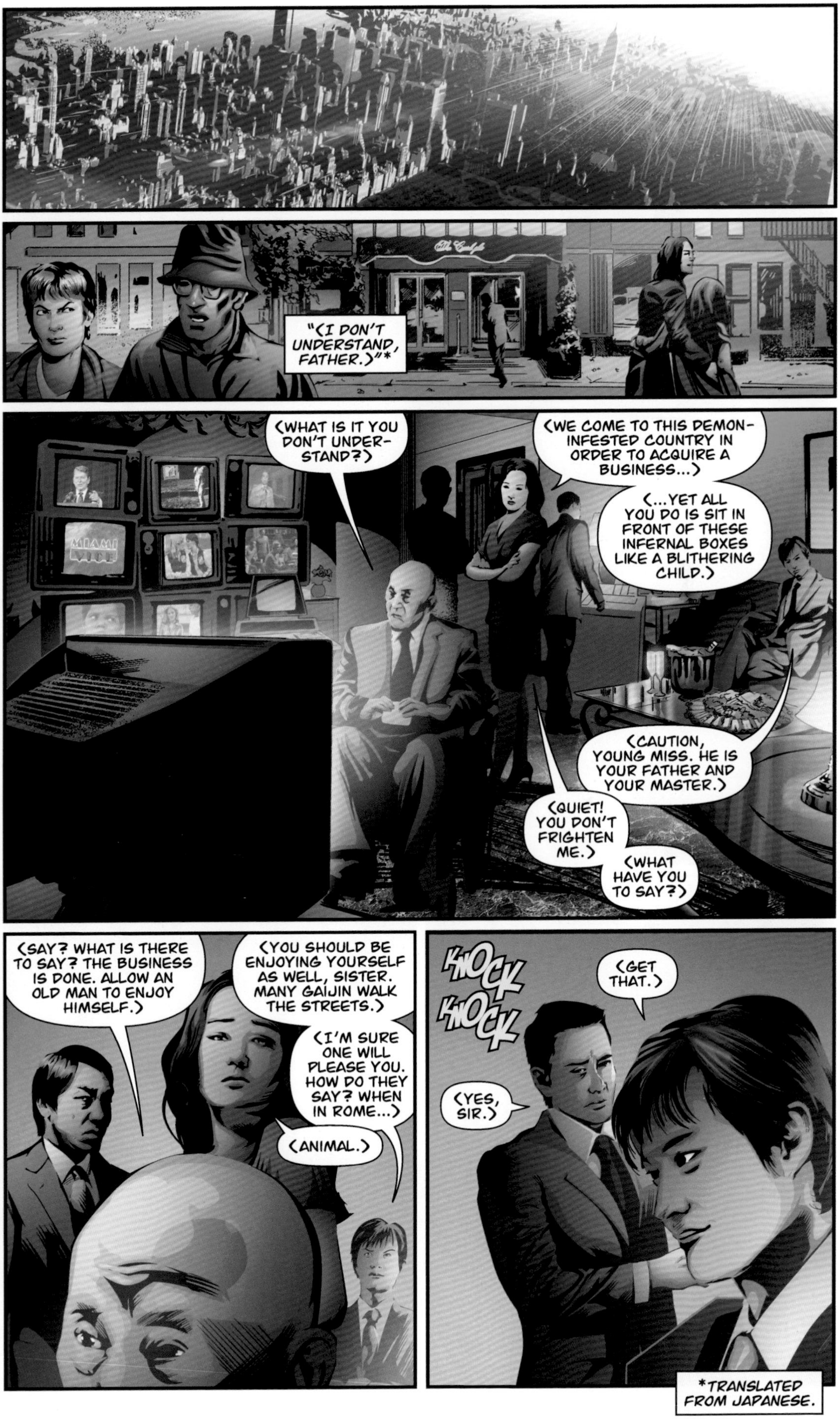

"(I DON'T UNDERSTAND, FATHER.)"*
(WHAT IS IT YOU DON'T UNDERSTAND?)
(WE COME TO THIS DEMON-INFESTED COUNTRY IN ORDER TO ACQUIRE A BUSINESS...)
(...YET ALL YOU DO IS SIT IN FRONT OF THESE INFERNAL BOXES LIKE A BLITHERING CHILD.)
(CAUTION, YOUNG MISS. HE IS YOUR FATHER AND YOUR MASTER.)
(QUIET! YOU DON'T FRIGHTEN ME.)
(WHAT HAVE YOU TO SAY?)
(SAY? WHAT IS THERE TO SAY? THE BUSINESS IS DONE. ALLOW AN OLD MAN TO ENJOY HIMSELF.)
(YOU SHOULD BE ENJOYING YOURSELF AS WELL, SISTER. MANY GAIJIN WALK THE STREETS.)
(I'M SURE ONE WILL PLEASE YOU. HOW DO THEY SAY? WHEN IN ROME...)
(ANIMAL.)
KNOCK KNOCK
(GET THAT.)
(YES, SIR.)


*TRANSLATED FROM JAPANESE.

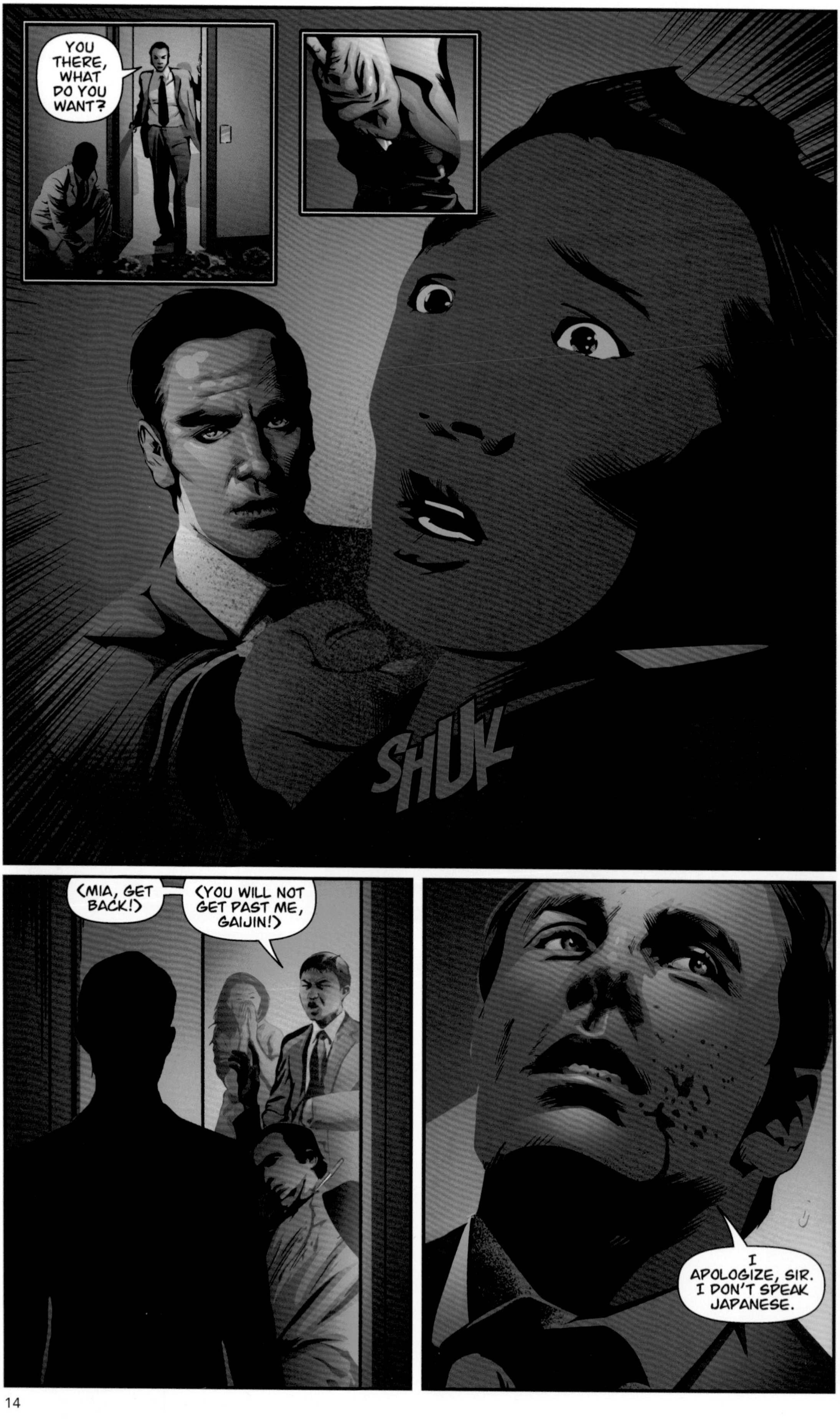
YOU THERE, WHAT DO YOU WANT?
SHUK
<MIA, GET BACK!>
<YOU WILL NOT GET PAST ME, GAIJIN!>
I APOLOGIZE, SIR. I DON'T SPEAK JAPANESE.

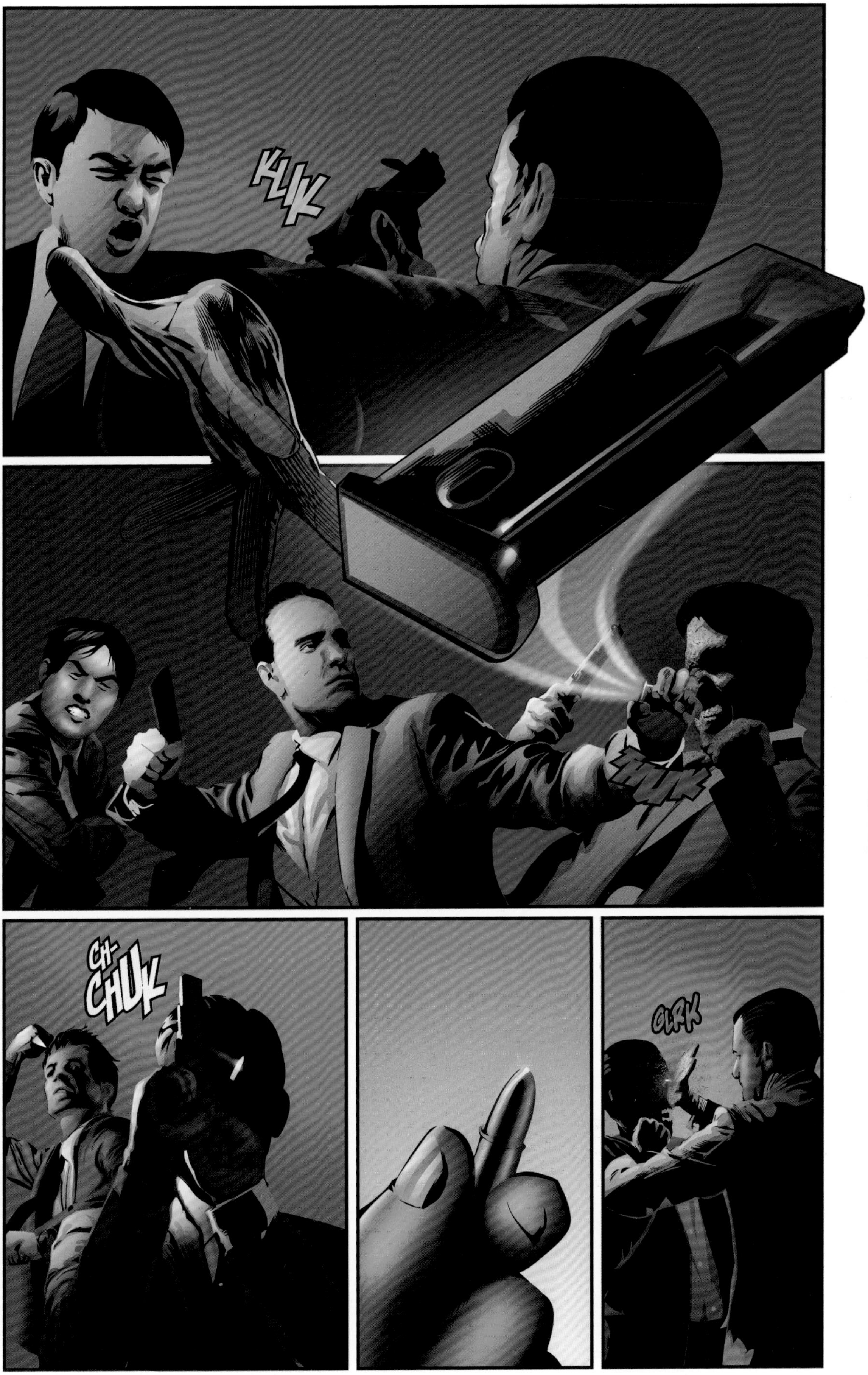
KLIK
THUK
CH-CHUK
GLRK

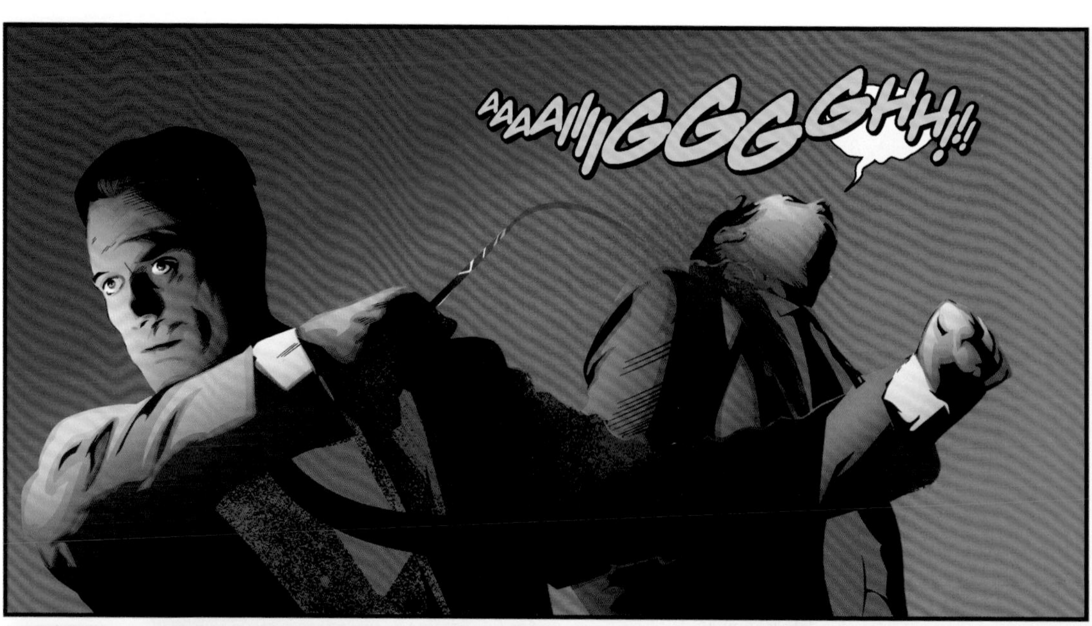
AAAAIIIIGGGGGHH!!

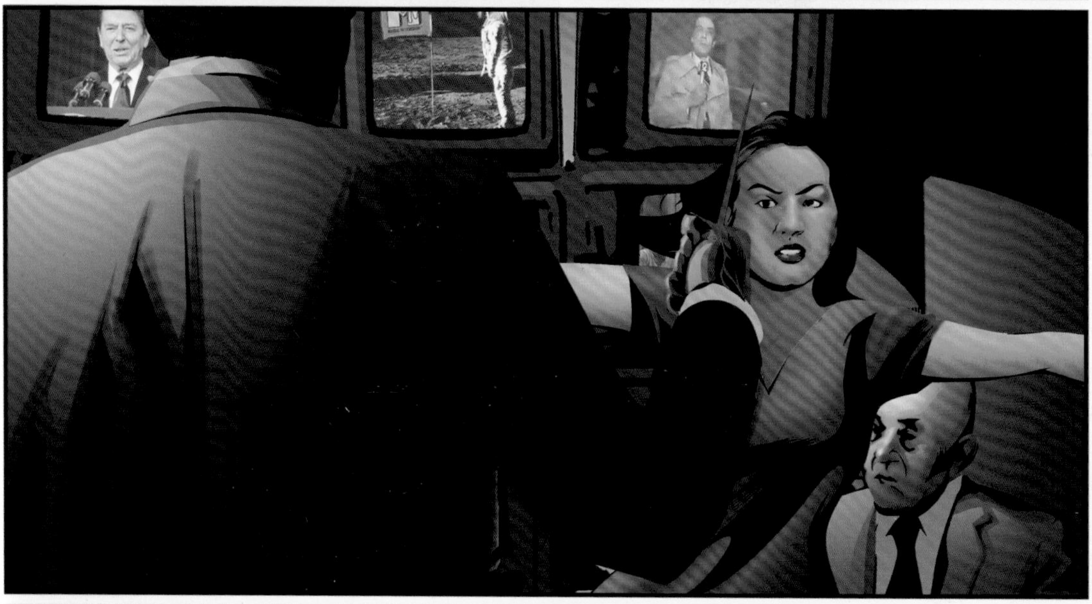

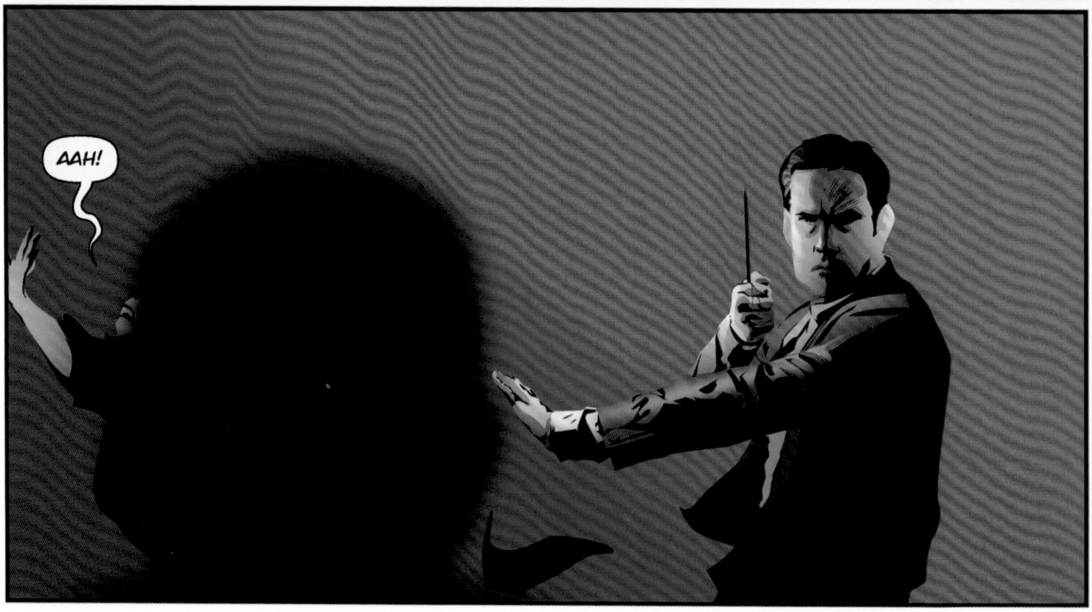
AAH!

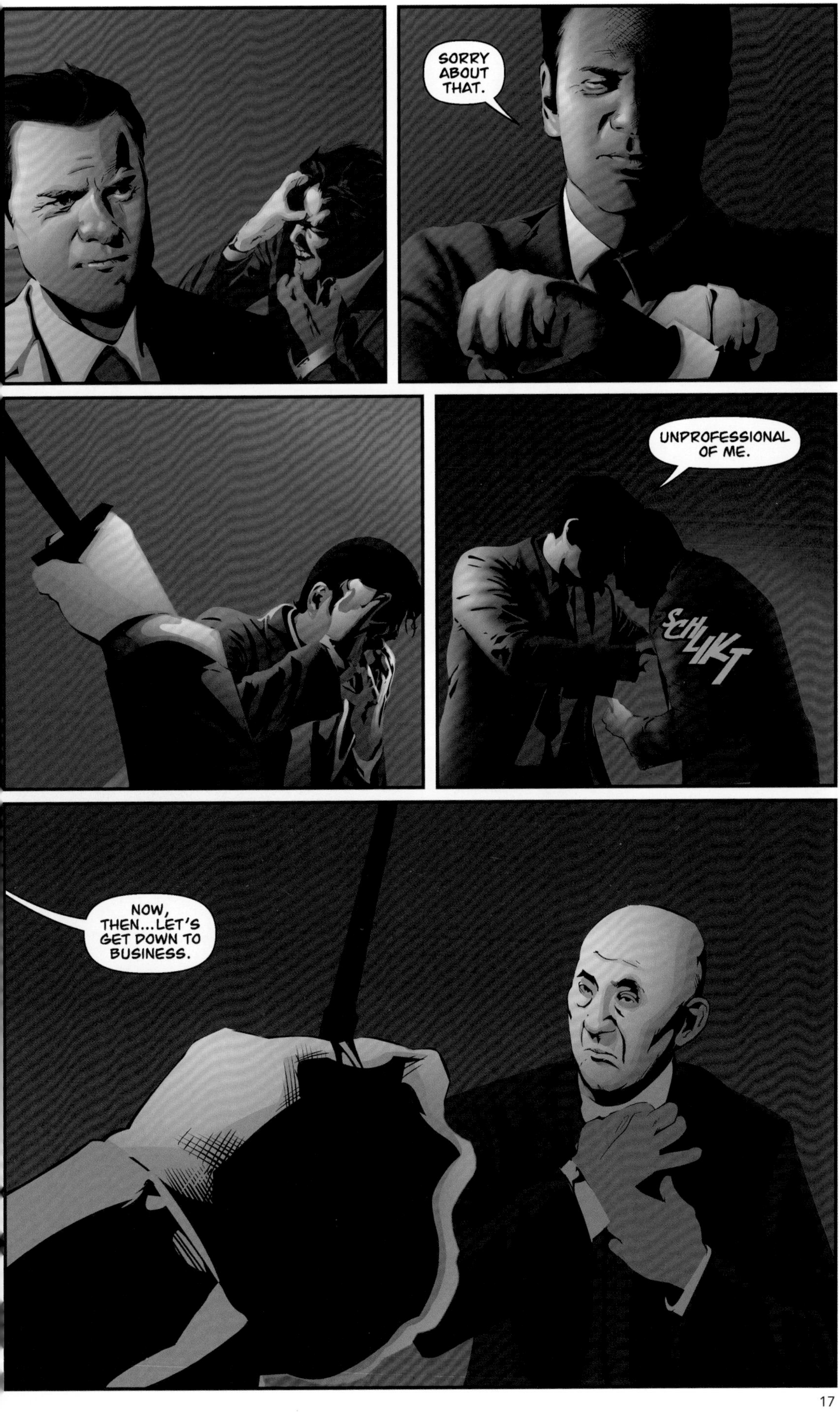
SORRY ABOUT THAT.
UNPROFESSIONAL OF ME.
SCHLIKT
NOW, THEN...LET'S GET DOWN TO BUSINESS.

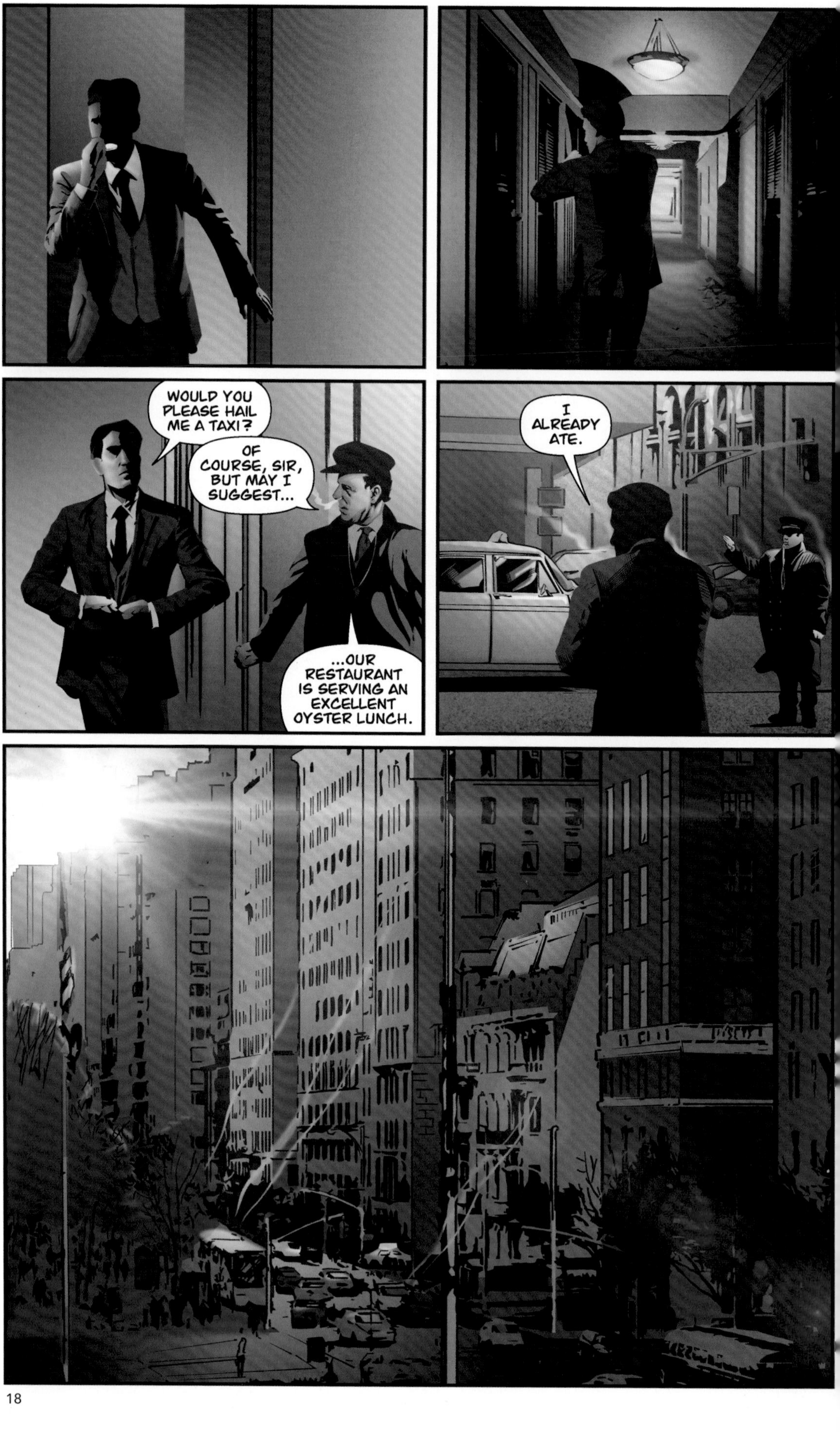
WOULD YOU PLEASE HAIL ME A TAXI?
OF COURSE, SIR, BUT MAY I SUGGEST...
...OUR RESTAURANT IS SERVING AN EXCELLENT OYSTER LUNCH.
I ALREADY ATE.

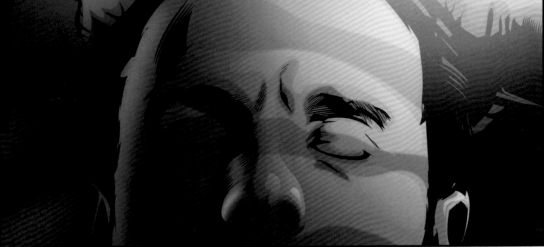

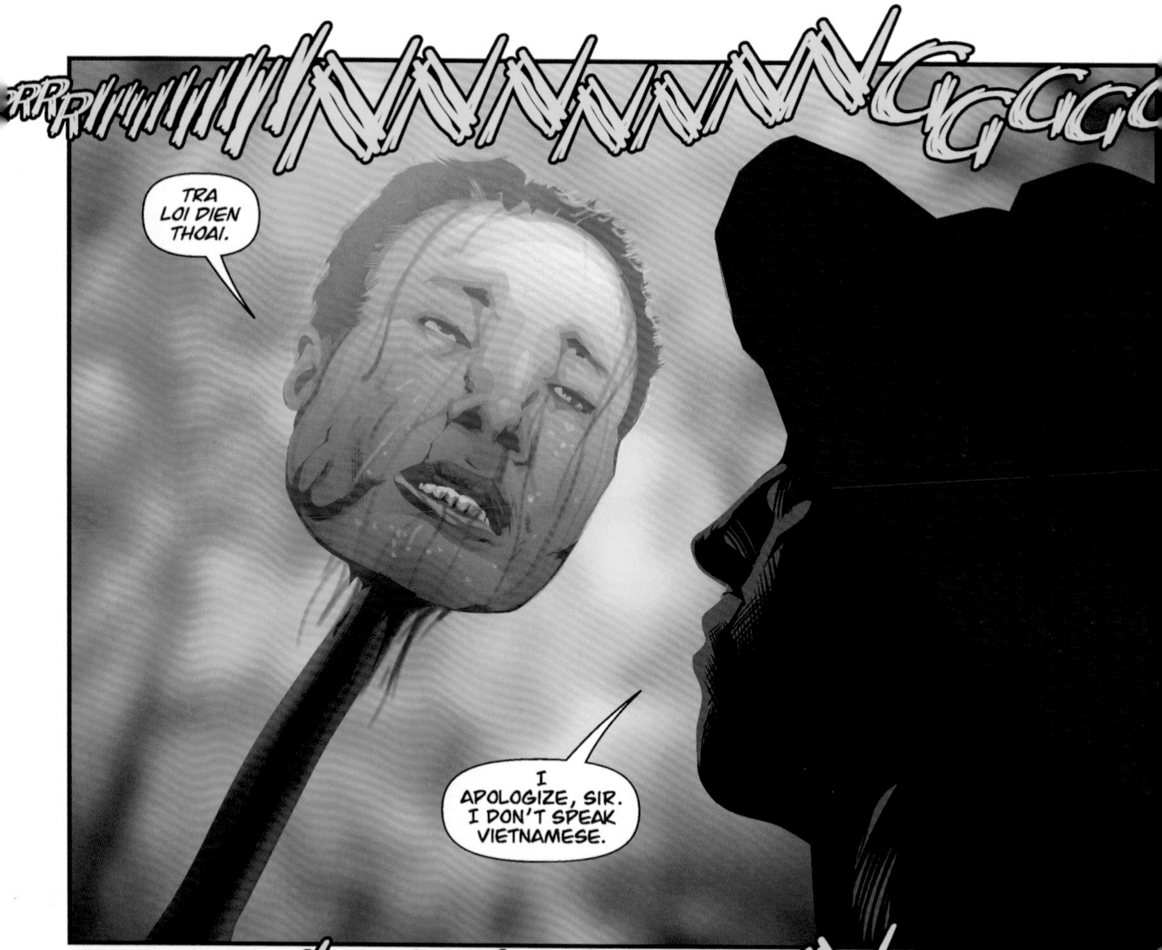
PRRRIIIIIIIIINNNNNNNNGGGG
TRA LOI DIEN THOAI.
I APOLOGIZE, SIR. I DON'T SPEAK VIETNAMESE.

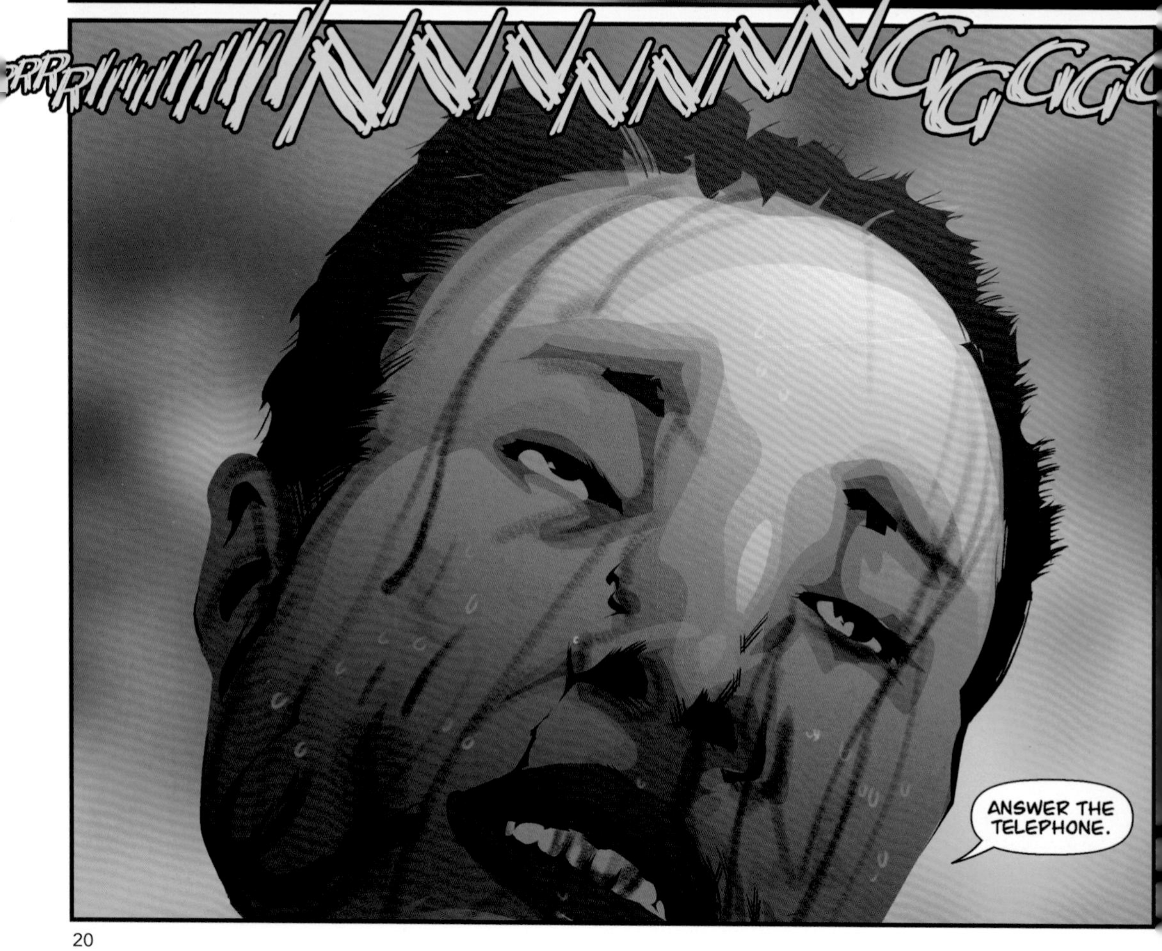
PRRRIIIIIIIIINNNNNNNNGGGG
ANSWER THE TELEPHONE.

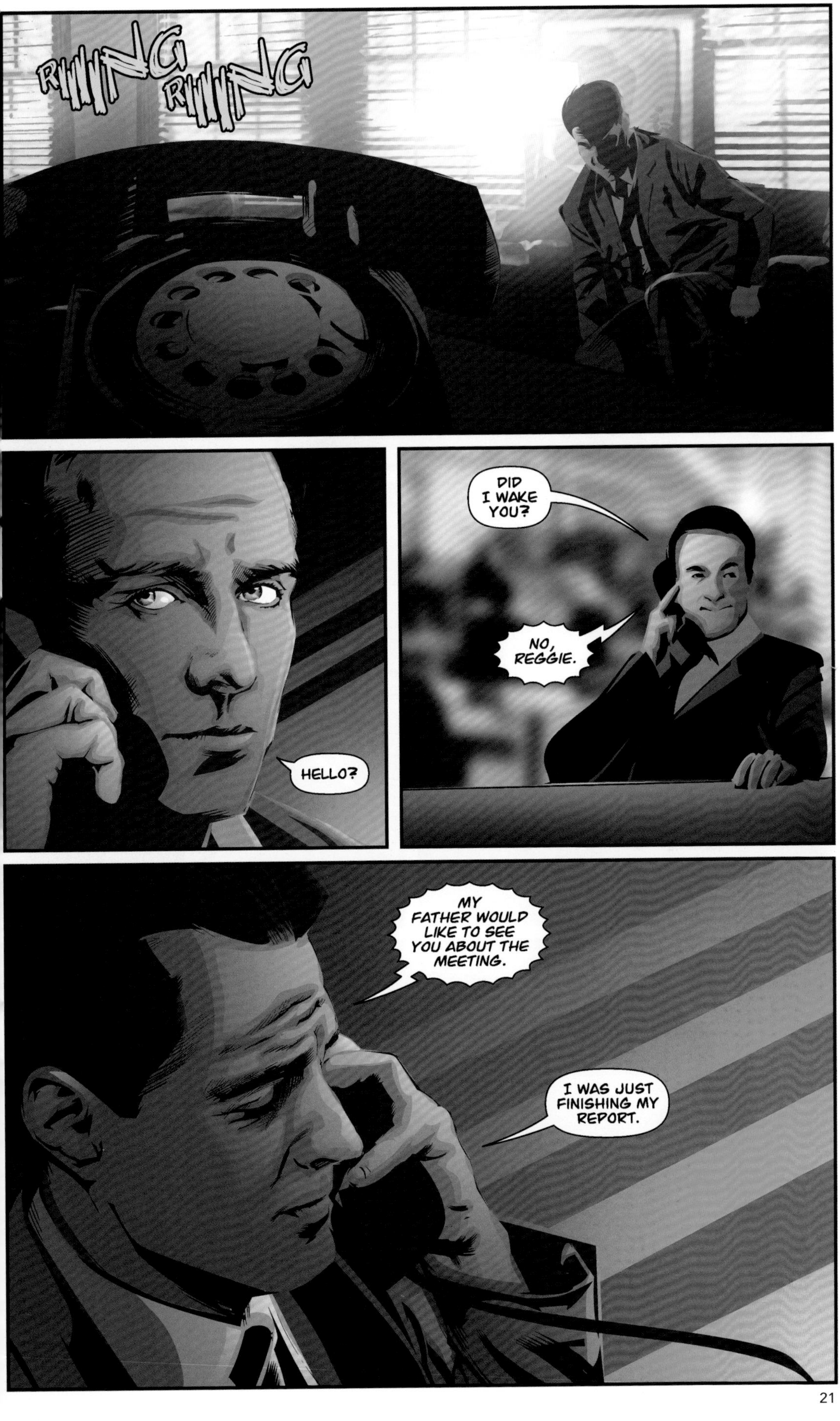
RING RING
DID I WAKE YOU?
HELLO?
NO, REGGIE.
MY FATHER WOULD LIKE TO SEE YOU ABOUT THE MEETING.
I WAS JUST FINISHING MY REPORT.

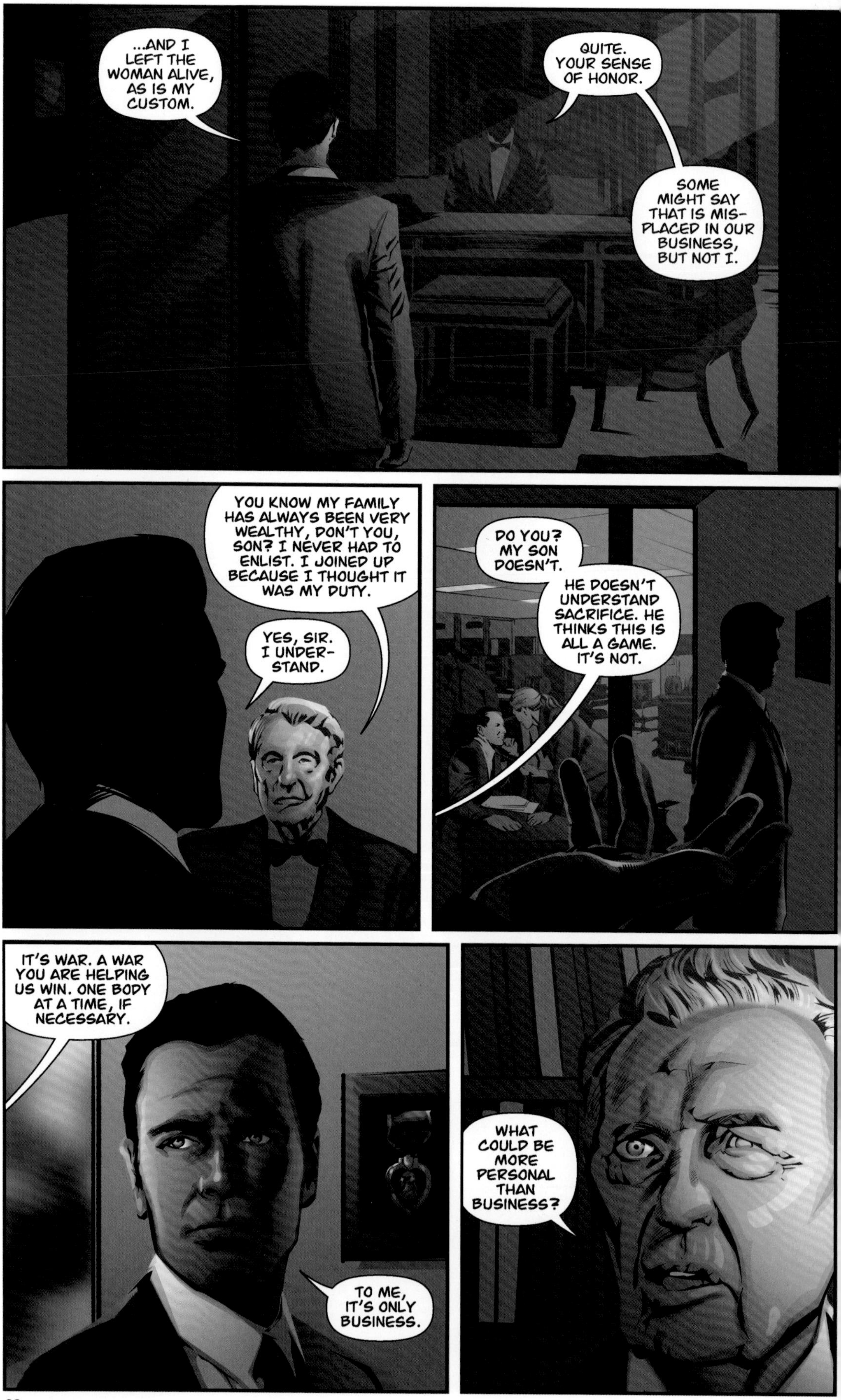
...AND I LEFT THE WOMAN ALIVE, AS IS MY CUSTOM.
QUITE. YOUR SENSE OF HONOR.
SOME MIGHT SAY THAT IS MIS-PLACED IN OUR BUSINESS, BUT NOT I.
YOU KNOW MY FAMILY HAS ALWAYS BEEN VERY WEALTHY, DON'T YOU, SON? I NEVER HAD TO ENLIST. I JOINED UP BECAUSE I THOUGHT IT WAS MY DUTY.
YES, SIR. I UNDER-STAND.
DO YOU? MY SON DOESN'T.
HE DOESN'T UNDERSTAND SACRIFICE. HE THINKS THIS IS ALL A GAME. IT'S NOT.
IT'S WAR. A WAR YOU ARE HELPING US WIN. ONE BODY AT A TIME, IF NECESSARY.
TO ME, IT'S ONLY BUSINESS.
WHAT COULD BE MORE PERSONAL THAN BUSINESS?

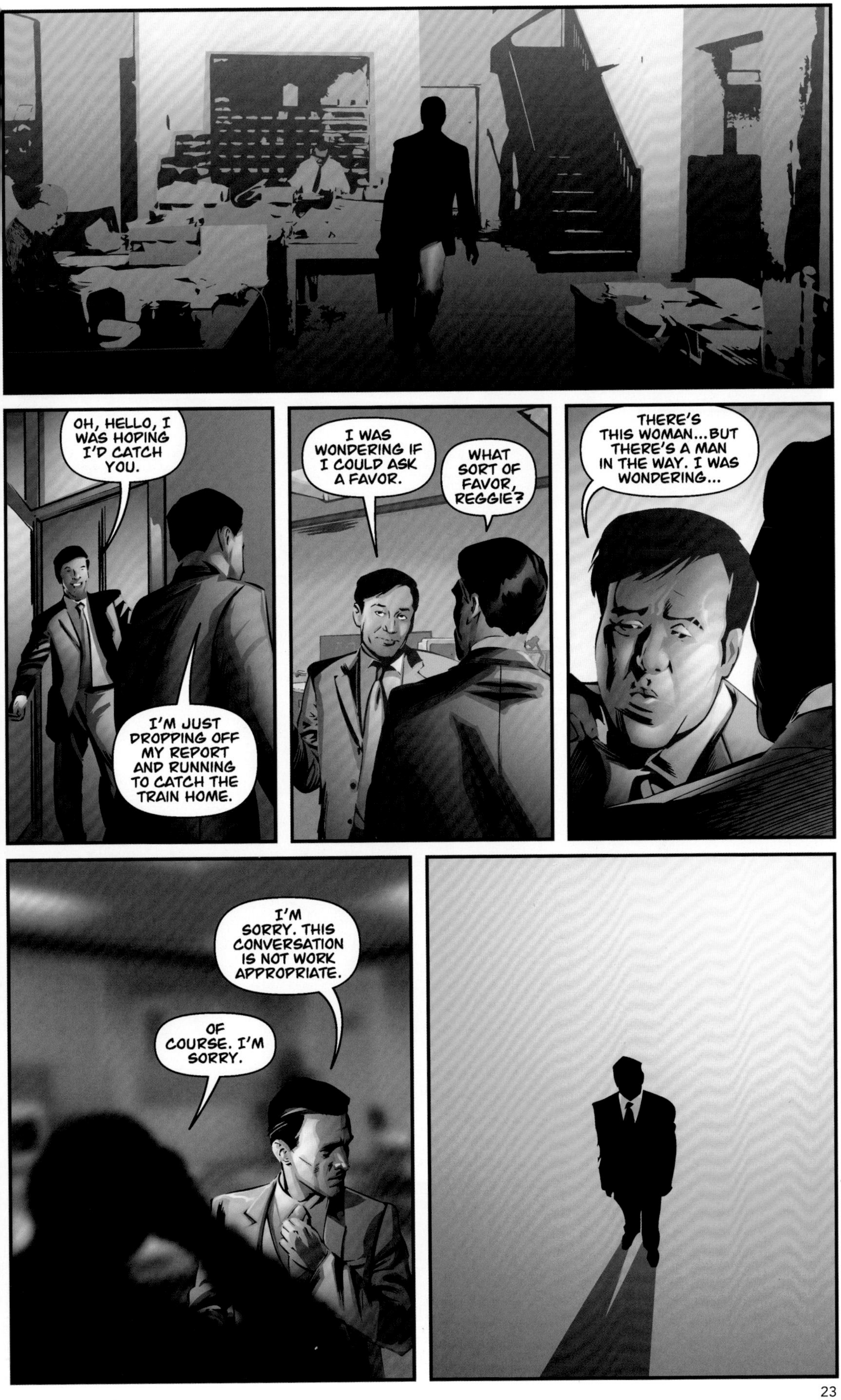

OH, HELLO, I WAS HOPING I'D CATCH YOU.
I'M JUST DROPPING OFF MY REPORT AND RUNNING TO CATCH THE TRAIN HOME.
I WAS WONDERING IF I COULD ASK A FAVOR.
WHAT SORT OF FAVOR, REGGIE?
THERE'S THIS WOMAN...BUT THERE'S A MAN IN THE WAY. I WAS WONDERING...
I'M SORRY. THIS CONVERSATION IS NOT WORK APPROPRIATE.
OF COURSE. I'M SORRY.

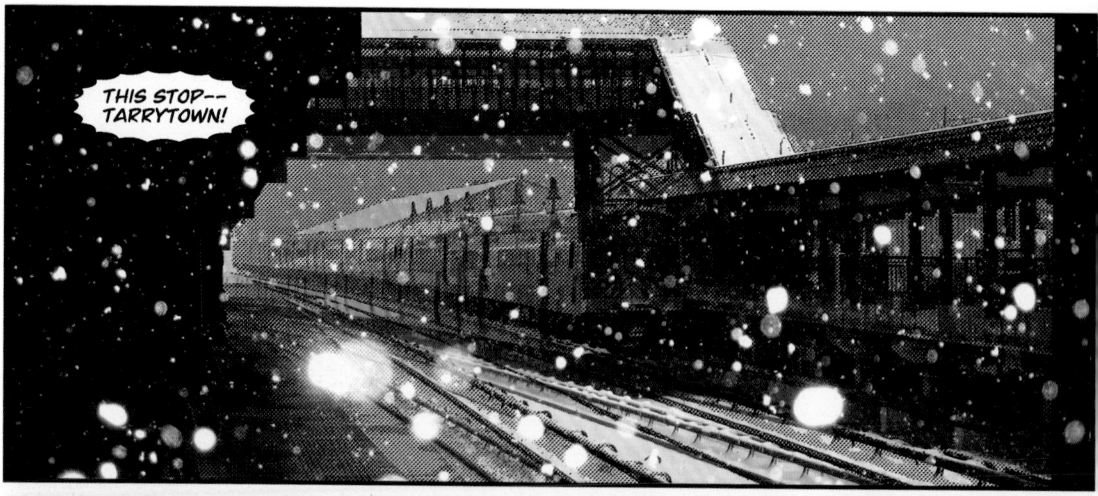
THIS STOP--
TARRYTOWN!

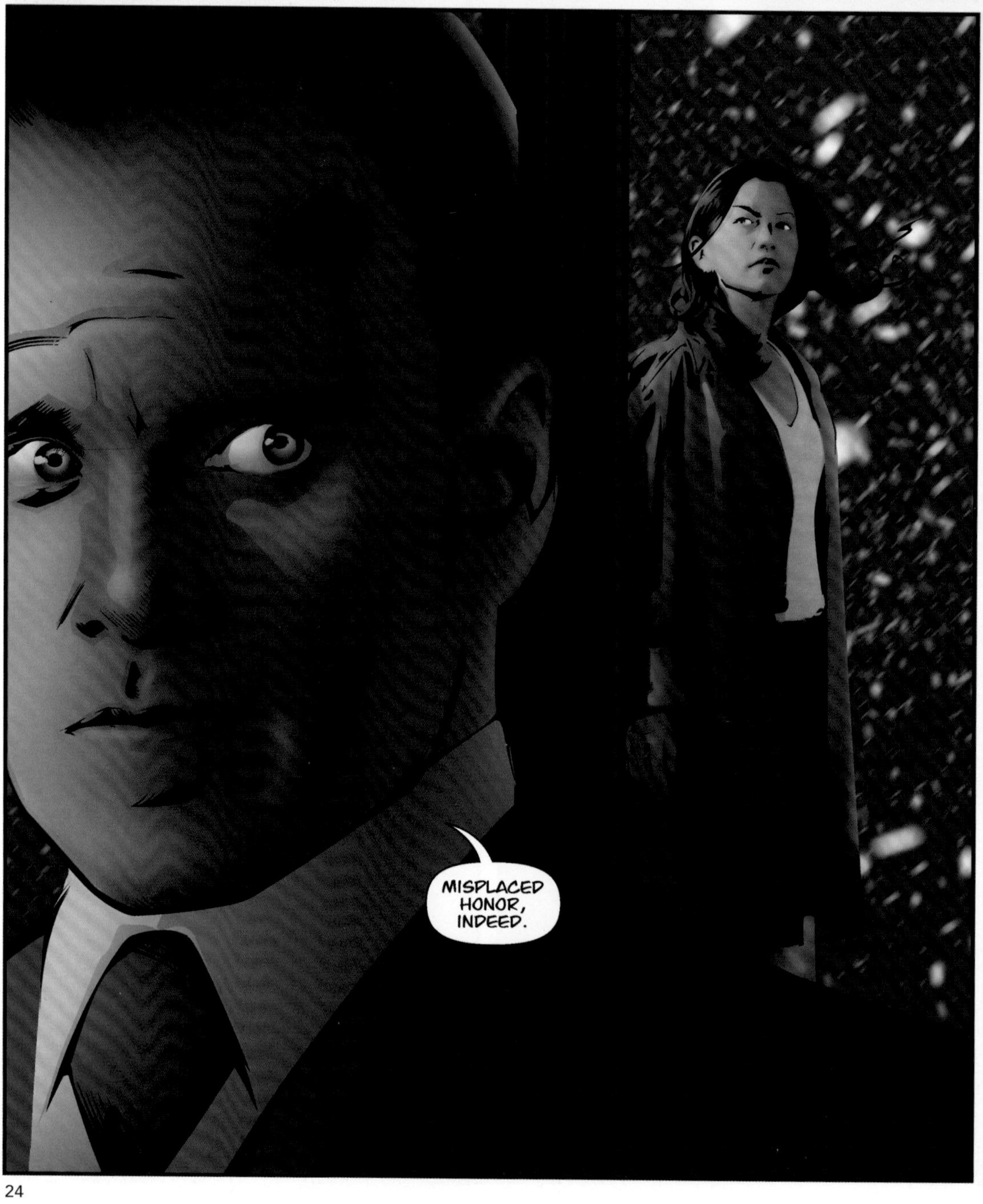
MISPLACED
HONOR,
INDEED.

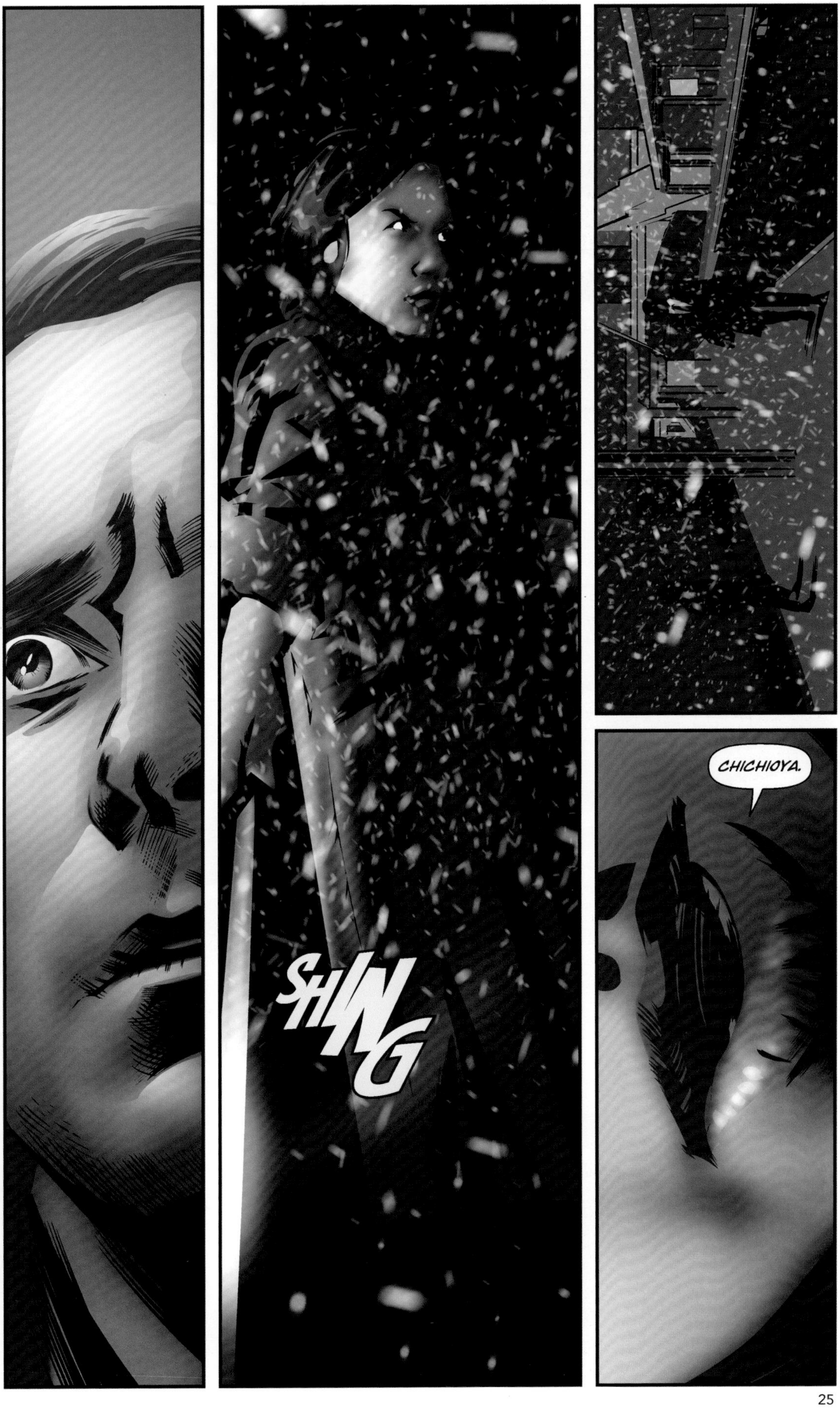
SHING
CHICHIOYA.

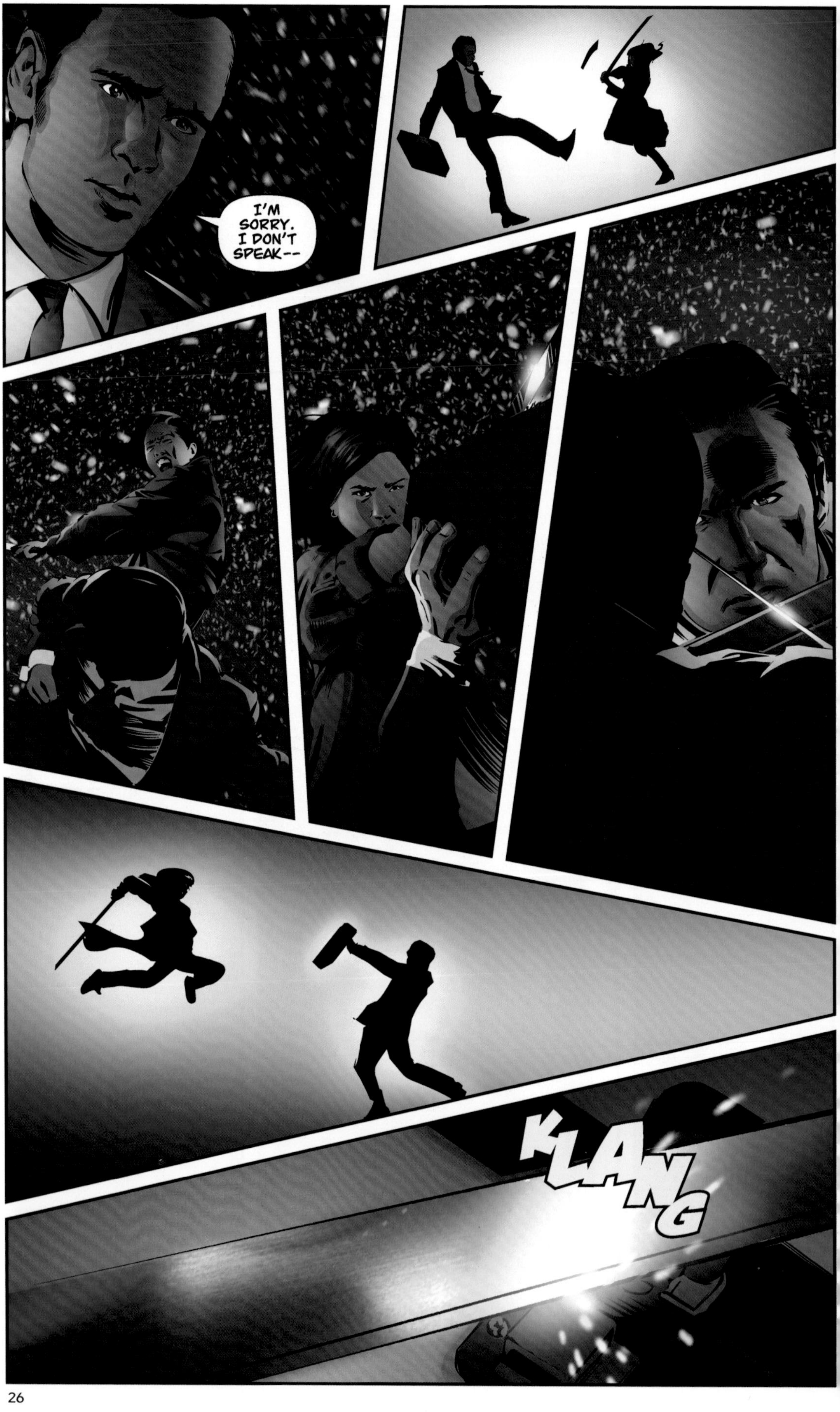
I'M SORRY. I DON'T SPEAK--
KLANG

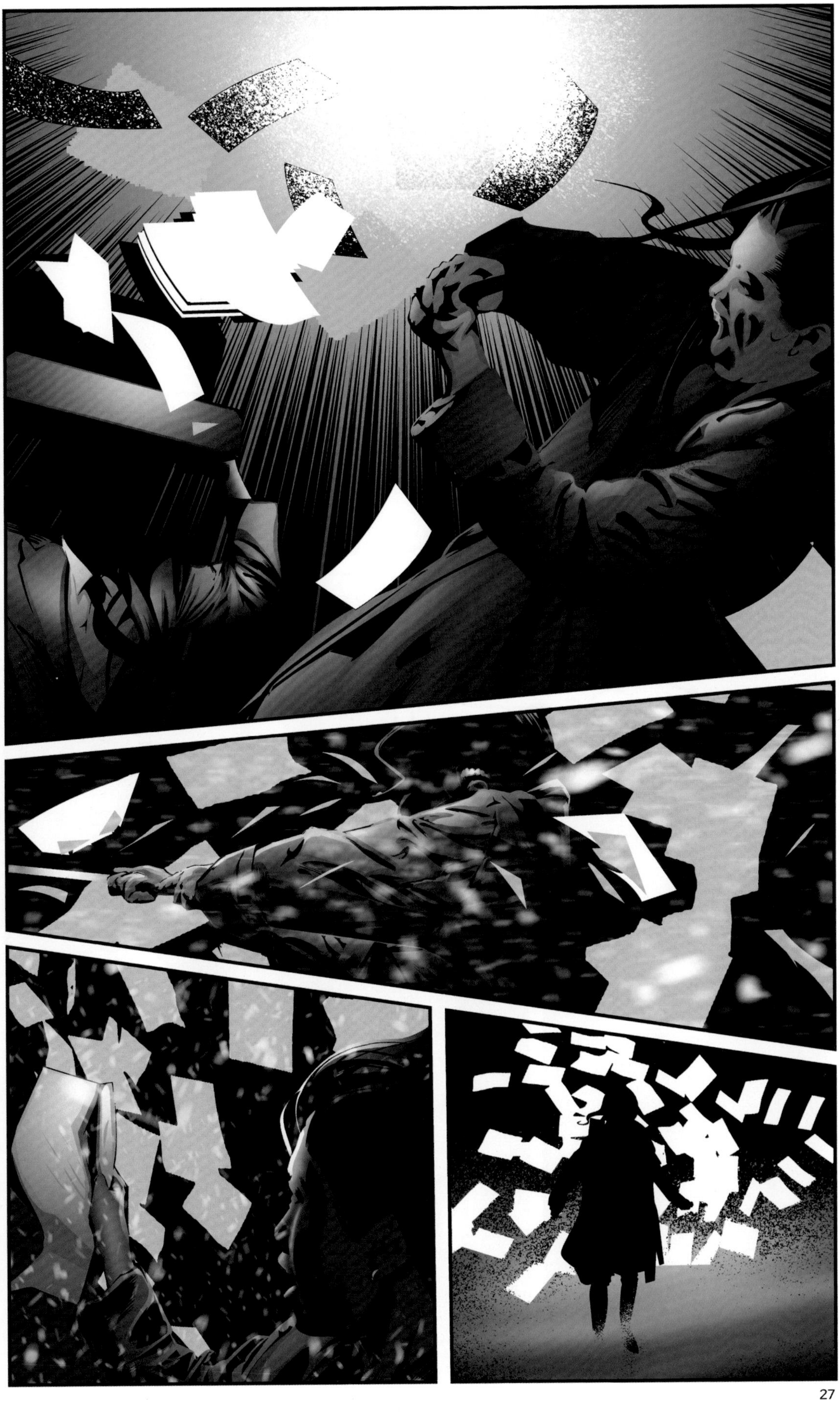

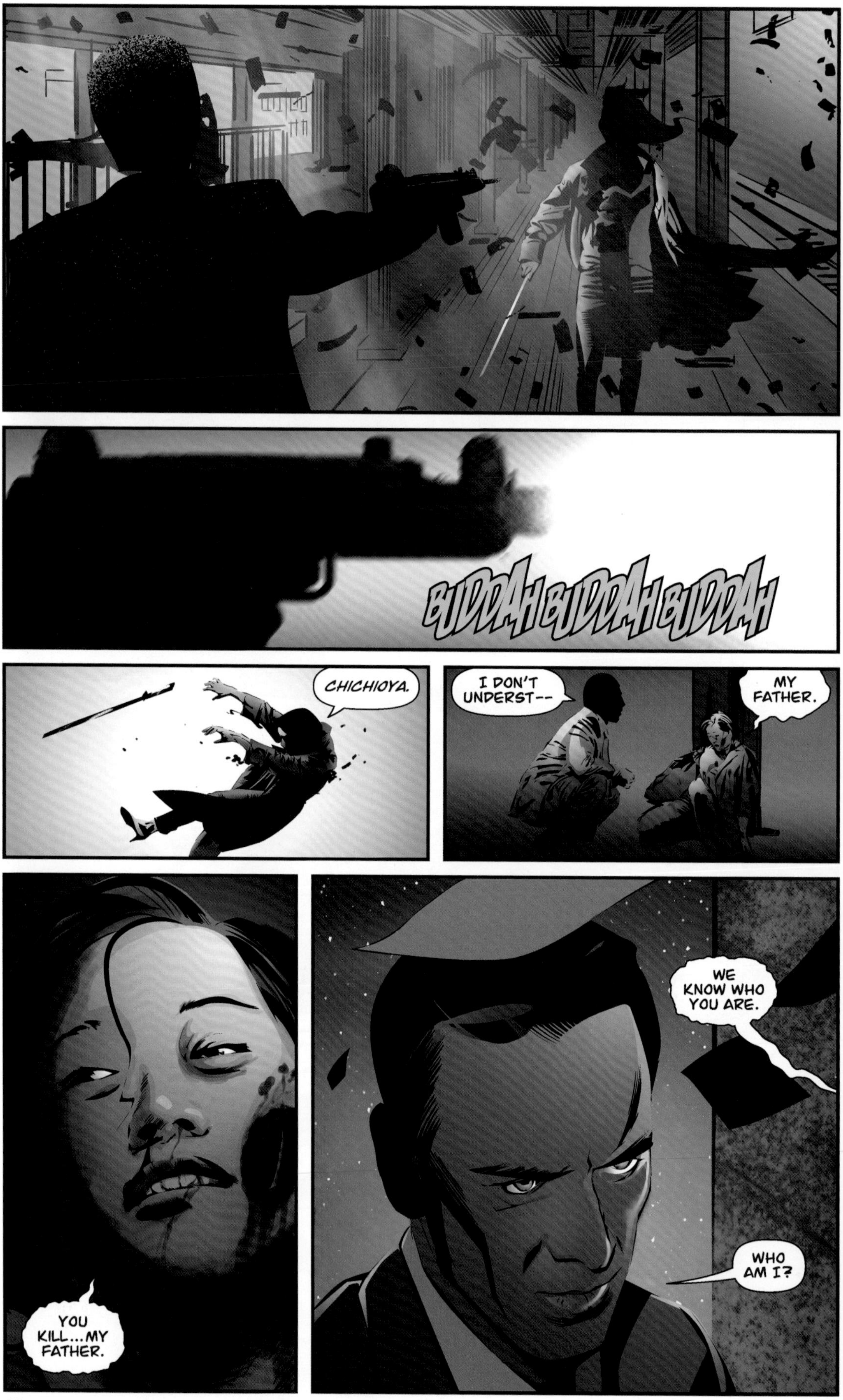
BUDDAH BUDDAH BUDDAH
CHICHIOYA.
I DON'T UNDERST--
MY FATHER.
YOU KILL...MY FATHER.
WE KNOW WHO YOU ARE.
WHO AM I?

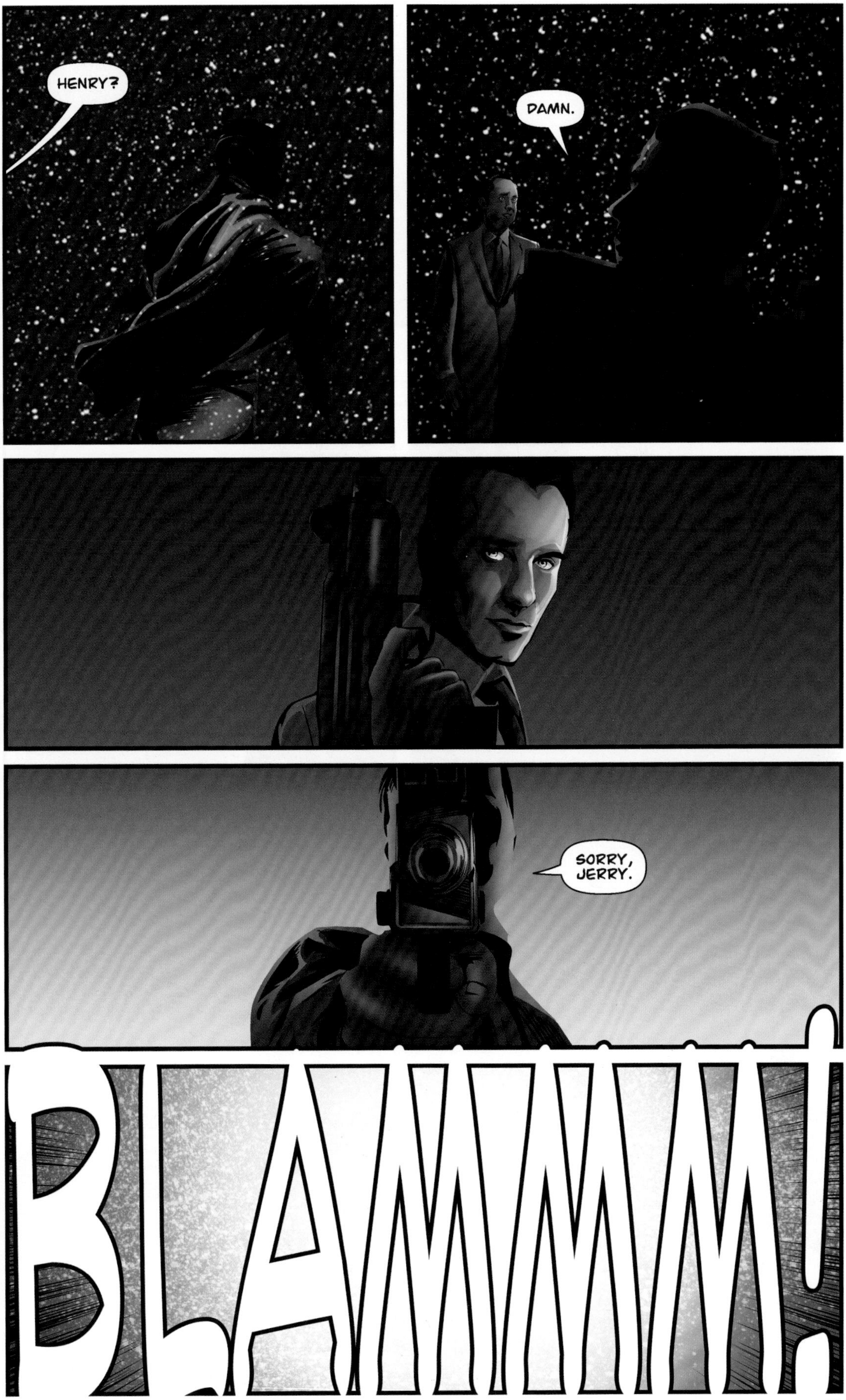
HENRY?
DAMN.
SORRY, JERRY.
BLAMMMM!

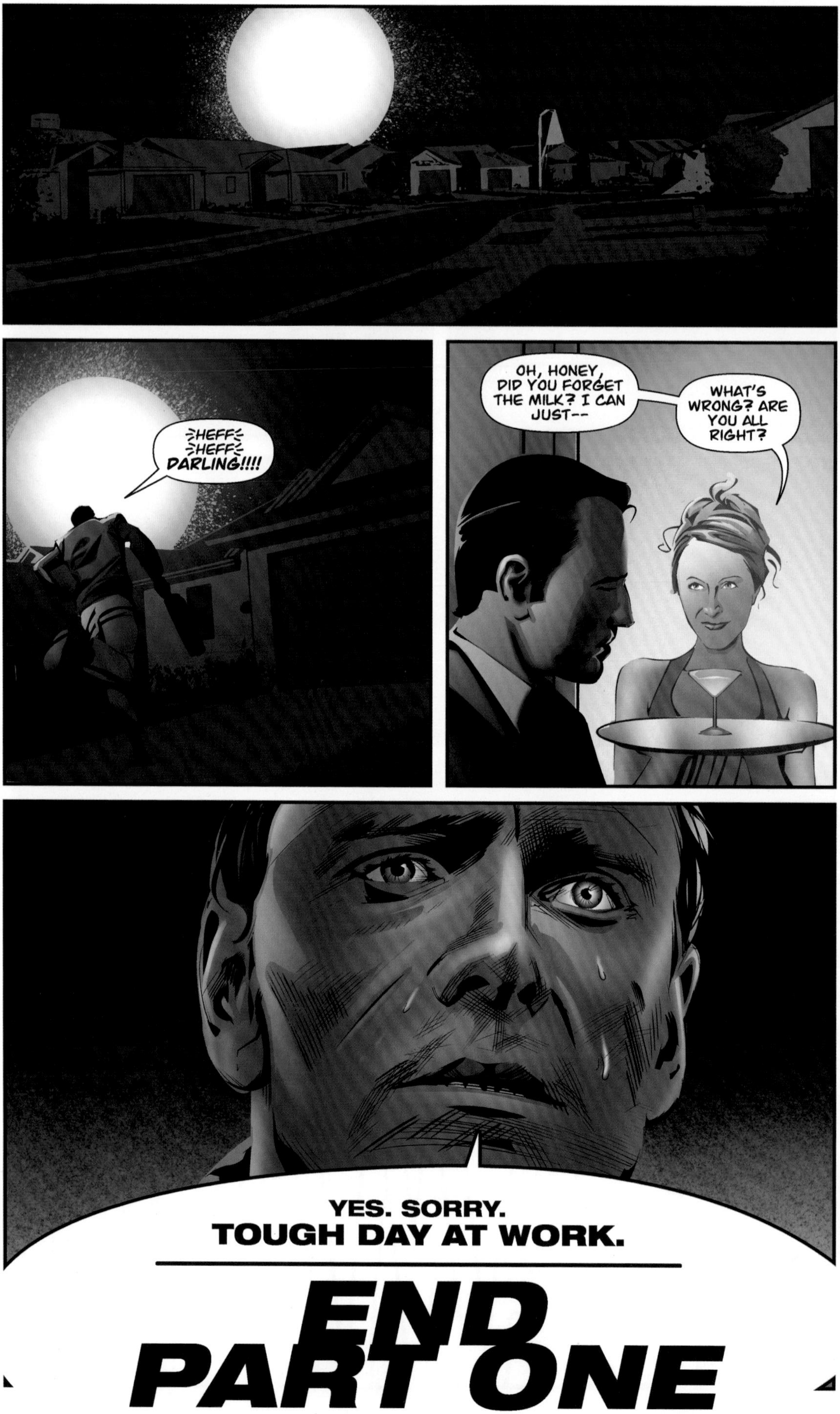

≷HEFF≶ ≷HEFF≶ DARLING!!!!
OH, HONEY, DID YOU FORGET THE MILK? I CAN JUST--
WHAT'S WRONG? ARE YOU ALL RIGHT?
YES. SORRY. TOUGH DAY AT WORK.
END PART ONE

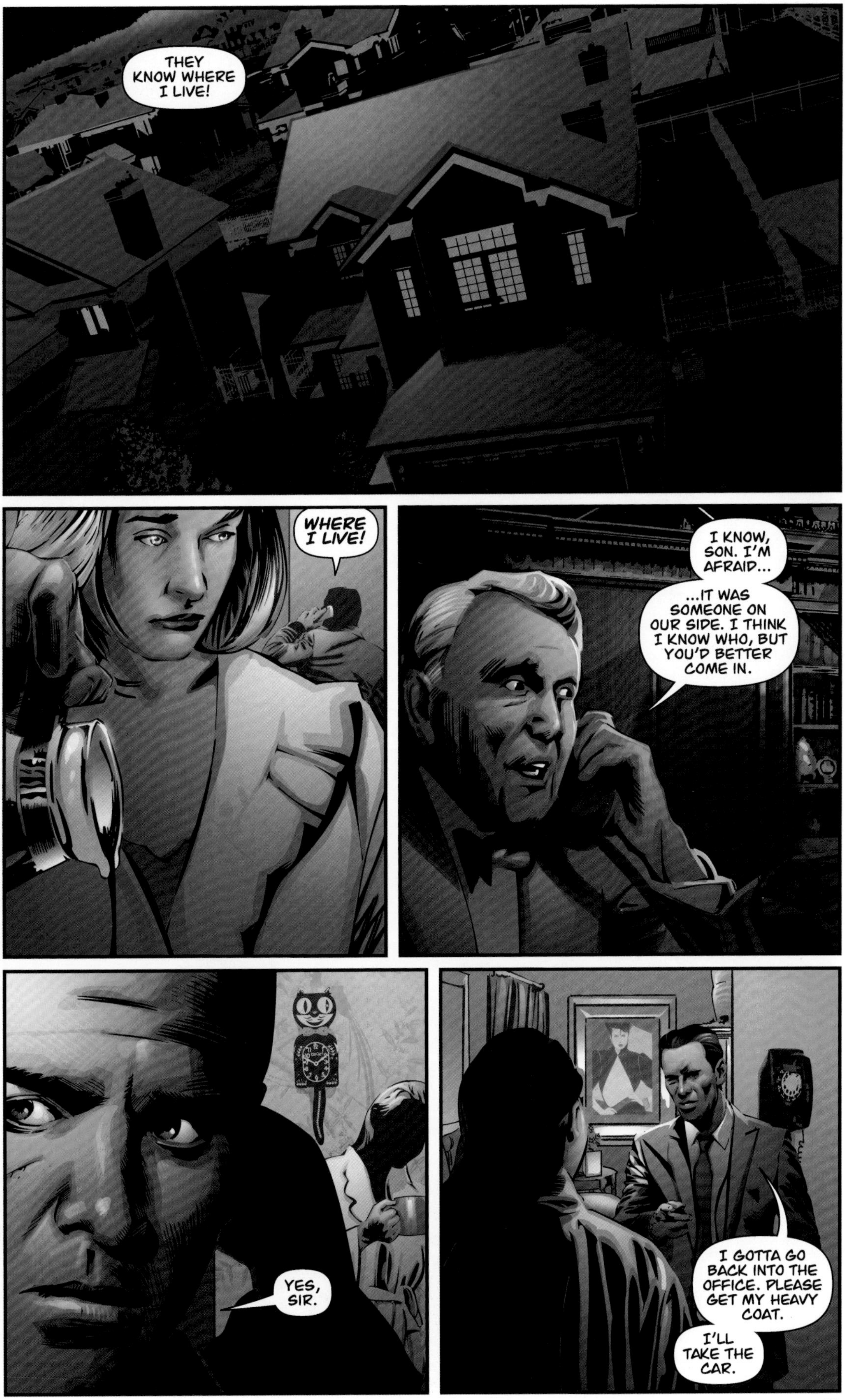
THEY KNOW WHERE I LIVE!
WHERE I LIVE!
I KNOW, SON. I'M AFRAID...
...IT WAS SOMEONE ON OUR SIDE. I THINK I KNOW WHO, BUT YOU'D BETTER COME IN.
YES, SIR.
I GOTTA GO BACK INTO THE OFFICE. PLEASE GET MY HEAVY COAT.
I'LL TAKE THE CAR.

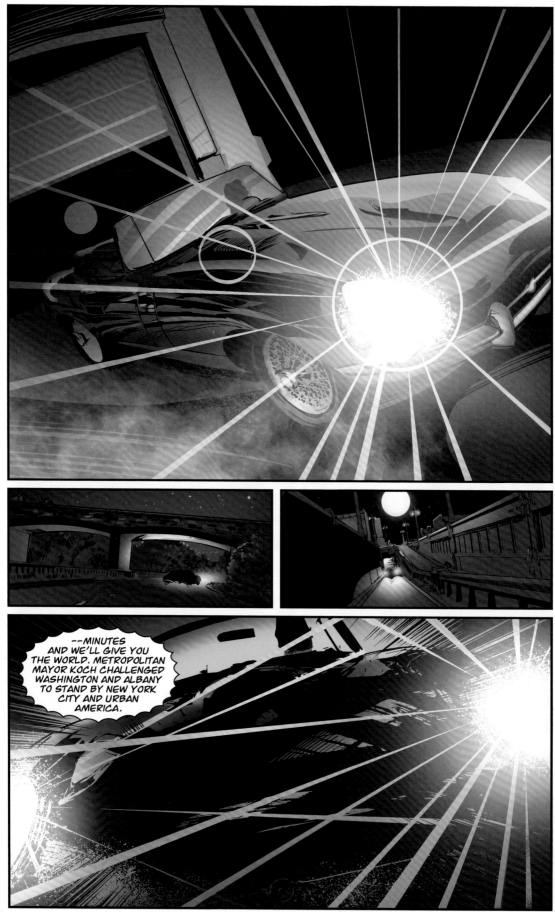

--MINUTES AND WE'LL GIVE YOU THE WORLD. METROPOLITAN MAYOR KOCH CHALLENGED WASHINGTON AND ALBANY TO STAND BY NEW YORK CITY AND URBAN AMERICA.

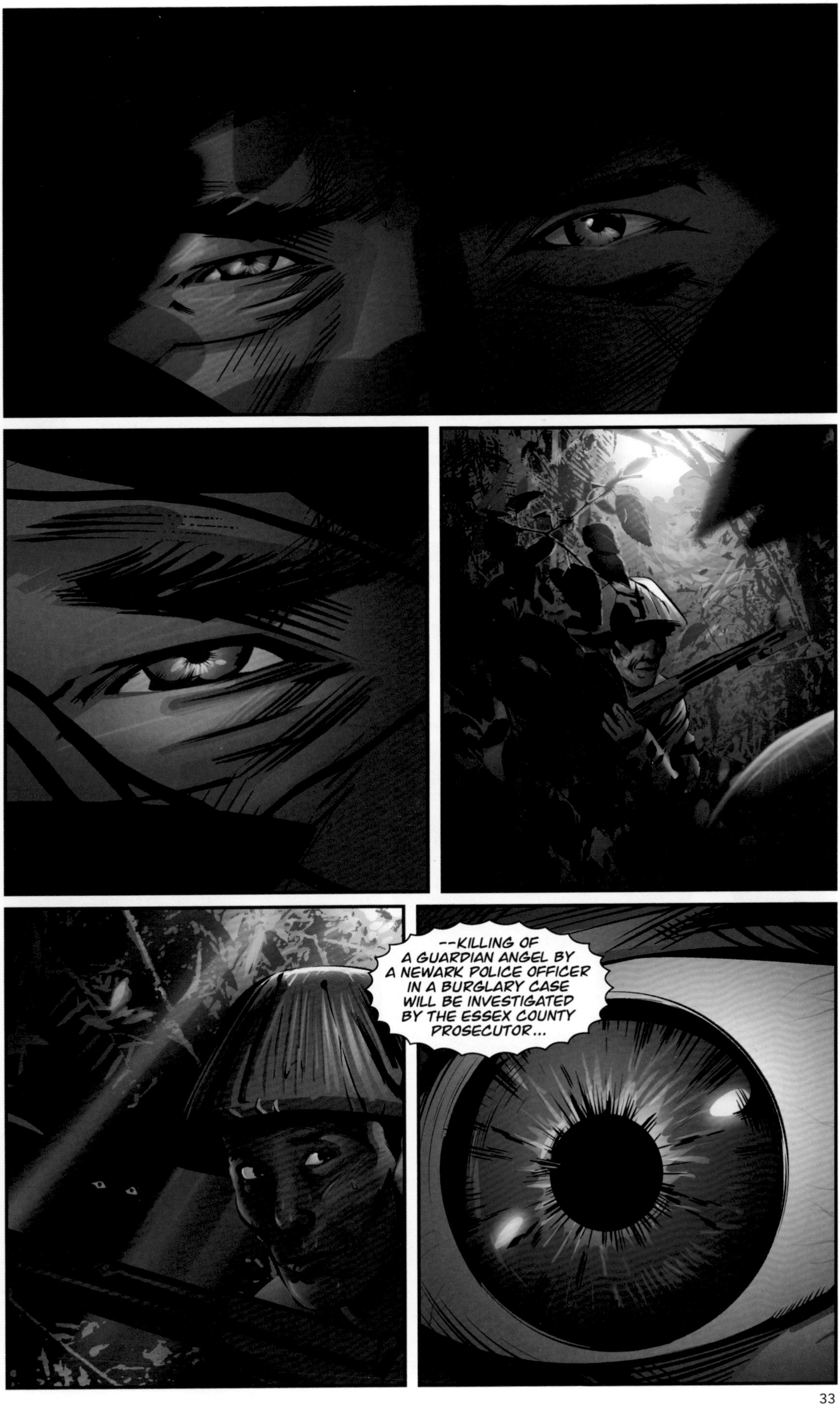
--KILLING OF A GUARDIAN ANGEL BY A NEWARK POLICE OFFICER IN A BURGLARY CASE WILL BE INVESTIGATED BY THE ESSEX COUNTY PROSECUTOR...

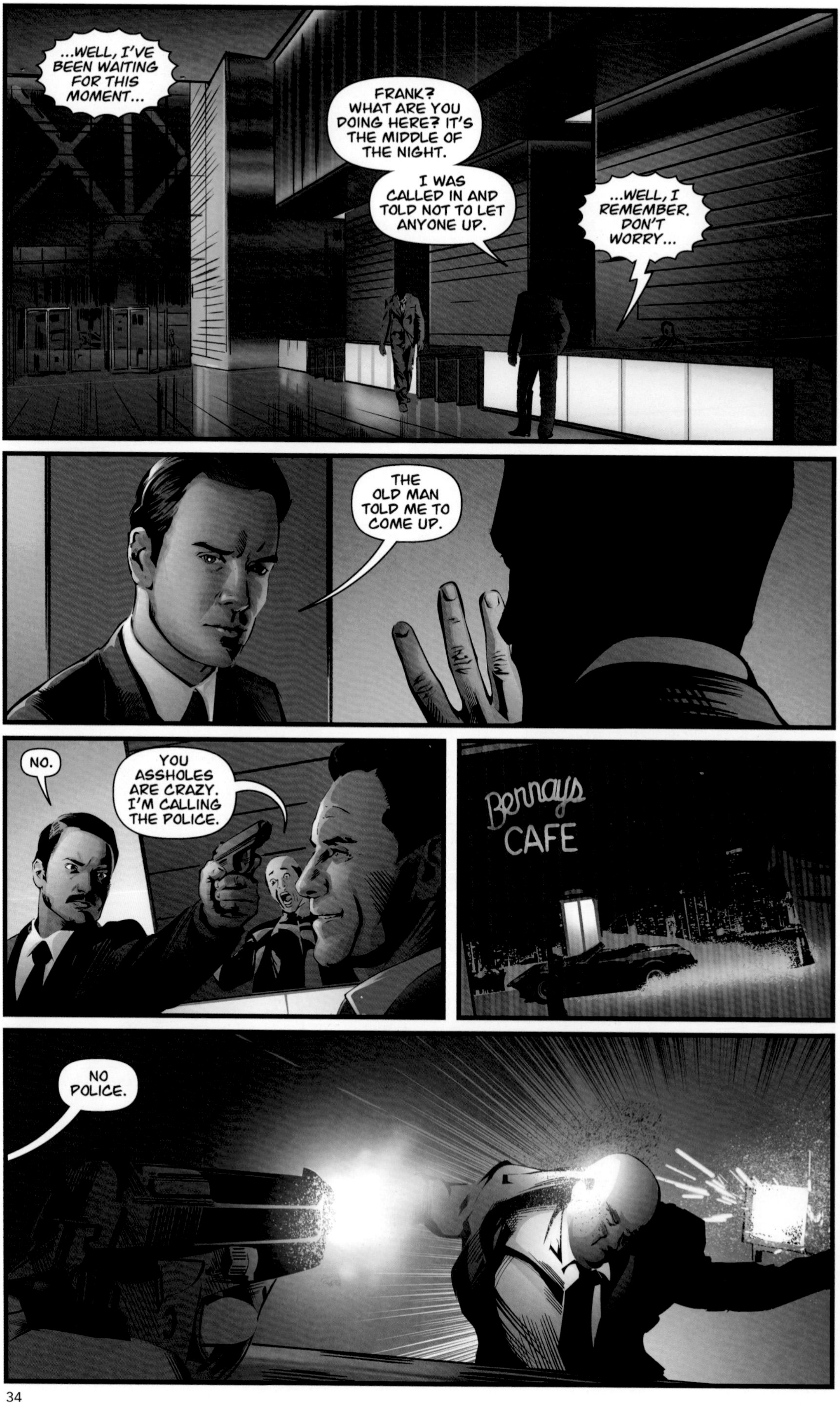
...WELL, I'VE BEEN WAITING FOR THIS MOMENT...
FRANK? WHAT ARE YOU DOING HERE? IT'S THE MIDDLE OF THE NIGHT.
I WAS CALLED IN AND TOLD NOT TO LET ANYONE UP.
...WELL, I REMEMBER. DON'T WORRY...
THE OLD MAN TOLD ME TO COME UP.
NO.
YOU ASSHOLES ARE CRAZY. I'M CALLING THE POLICE.
Bernays
CAFE
NO POLICE.

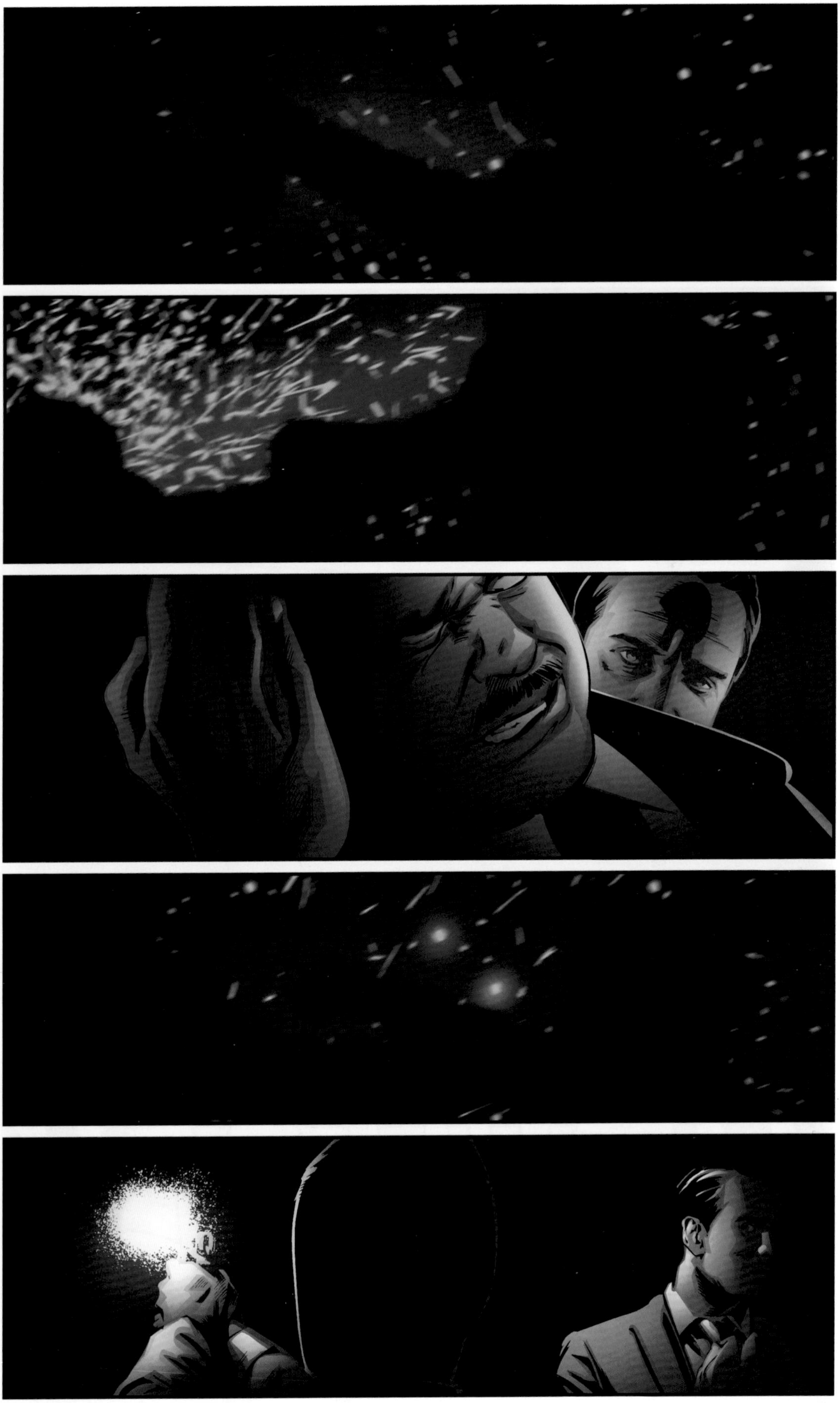

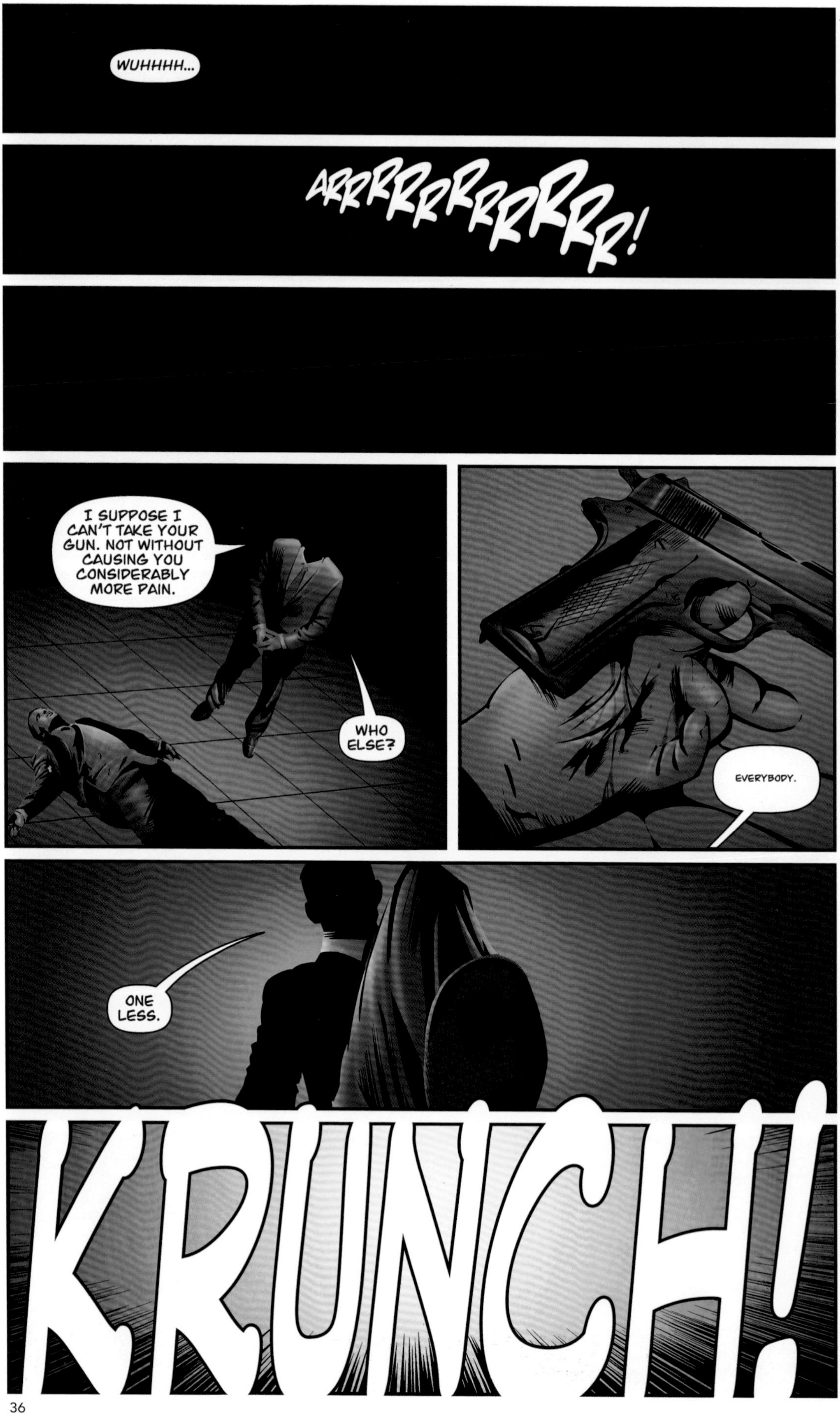
WUHHHH...
ARRRRRRRRRRRRR!
I SUPPOSE I CAN'T TAKE YOUR GUN. NOT WITHOUT CAUSING YOU CONSIDERABLY MORE PAIN.
WHO ELSE?
EVERYBODY.
ONE LESS.
KRUNCH!

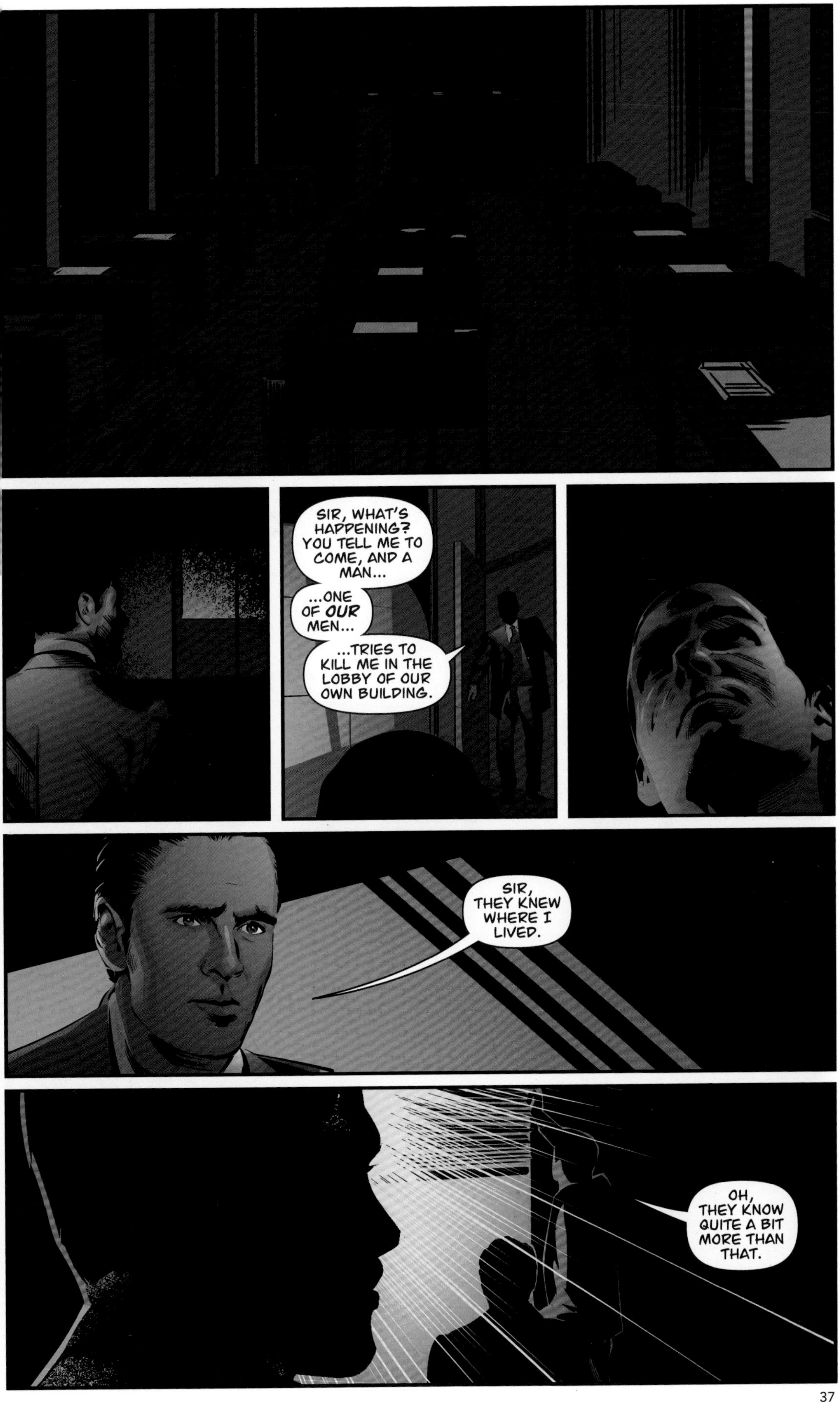
SIR, WHAT'S HAPPENING? YOU TELL ME TO COME, AND A MAN...
...ONE OF OUR MEN...
...TRIES TO KILL ME IN THE LOBBY OF OUR OWN BUILDING.
SIR, THEY KNEW WHERE I LIVED.
OH, THEY KNOW QUITE A BIT MORE THAN THAT.

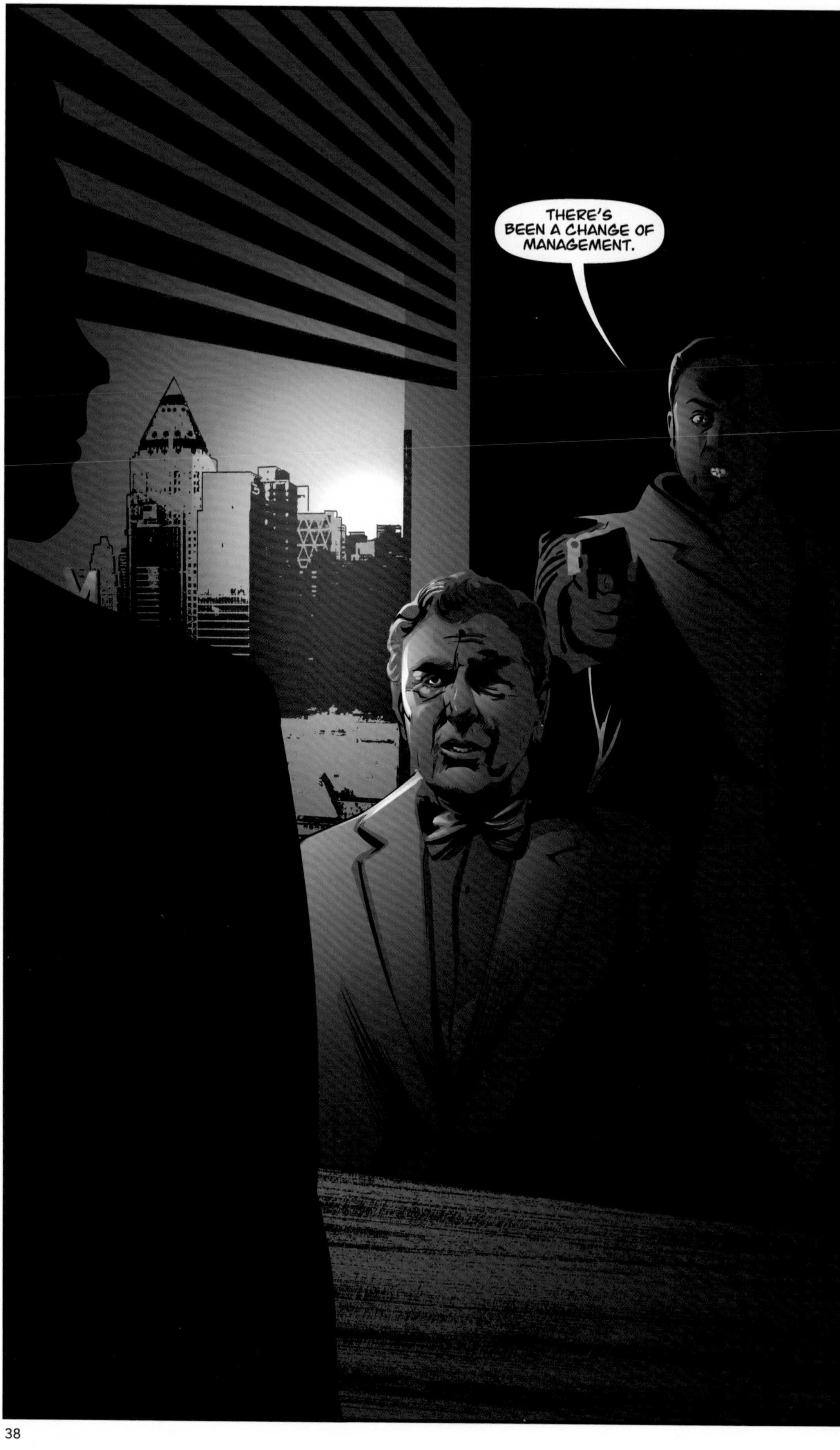
THERE'S BEEN A CHANGE OF MANAGEMENT.

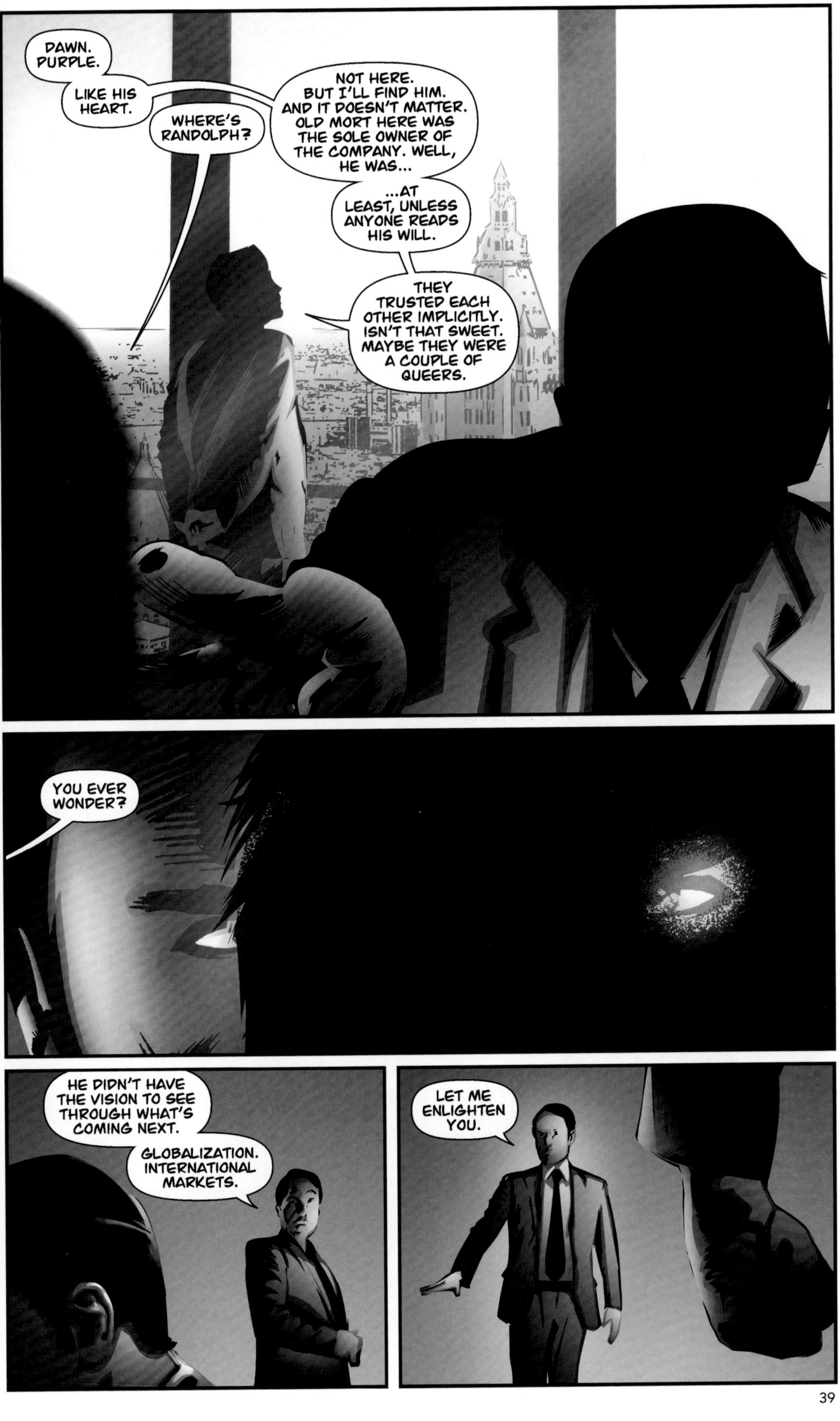
DAWN. PURPLE.
LIKE HIS HEART.
WHERE'S RANDOLPH?
NOT HERE. BUT I'LL FIND HIM. AND IT DOESN'T MATTER. OLD MORT HERE WAS THE SOLE OWNER OF THE COMPANY. WELL, HE WAS...
...AT LEAST, UNLESS ANYONE READS HIS WILL.
THEY TRUSTED EACH OTHER IMPLICITLY. ISN'T THAT SWEET. MAYBE THEY WERE A COUPLE OF QUEERS.
YOU EVER WONDER?
HE DIDN'T HAVE THE VISION TO SEE THROUGH WHAT'S COMING NEXT.
GLOBALIZATION. INTERNATIONAL MARKETS.
LET ME ENLIGHTEN YOU.

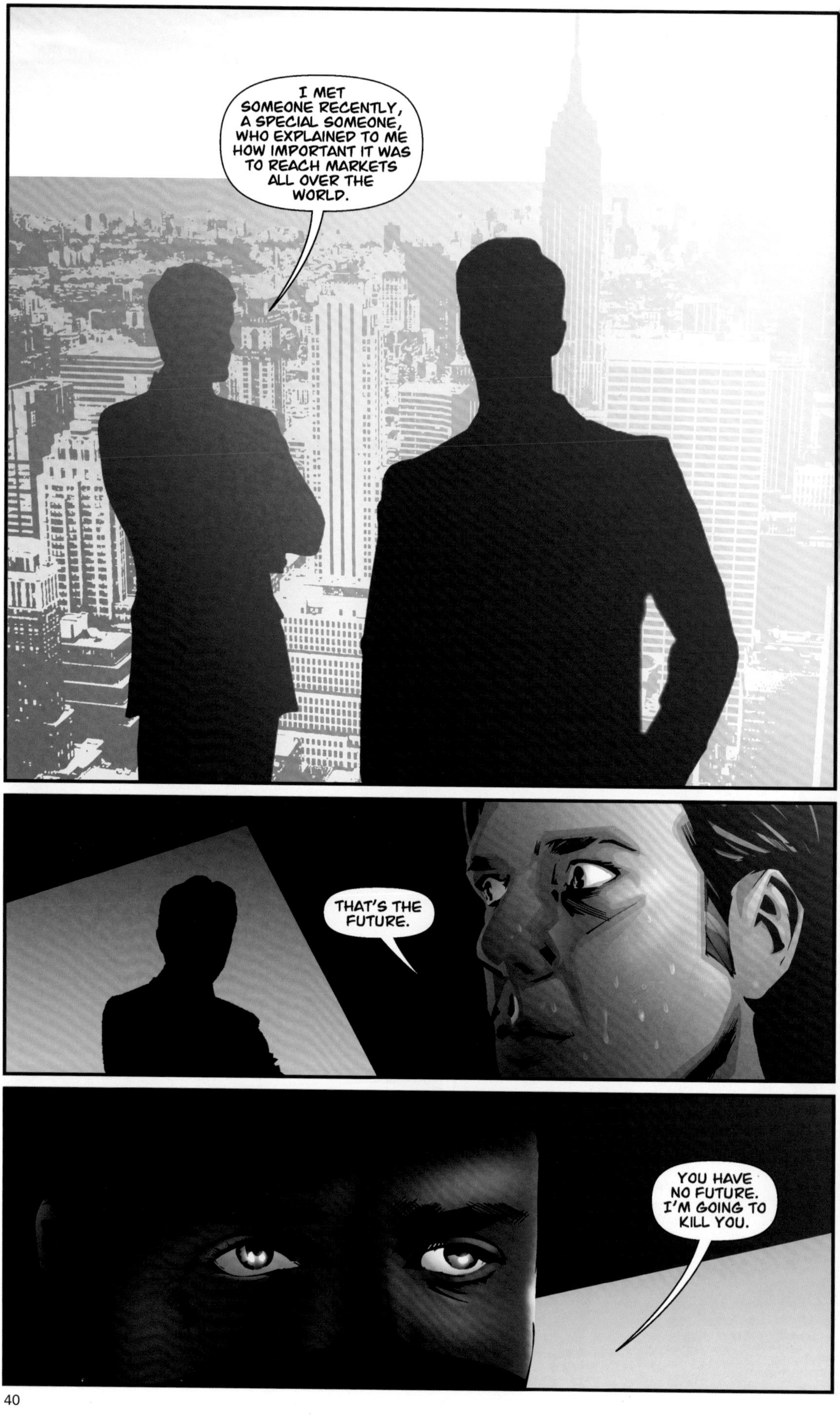
I MET SOMEONE RECENTLY, A SPECIAL SOMEONE, WHO EXPLAINED TO ME HOW IMPORTANT IT WAS TO REACH MARKETS ALL OVER THE WORLD.
THAT'S THE FUTURE.
YOU HAVE NO FUTURE. I'M GOING TO KILL YOU.

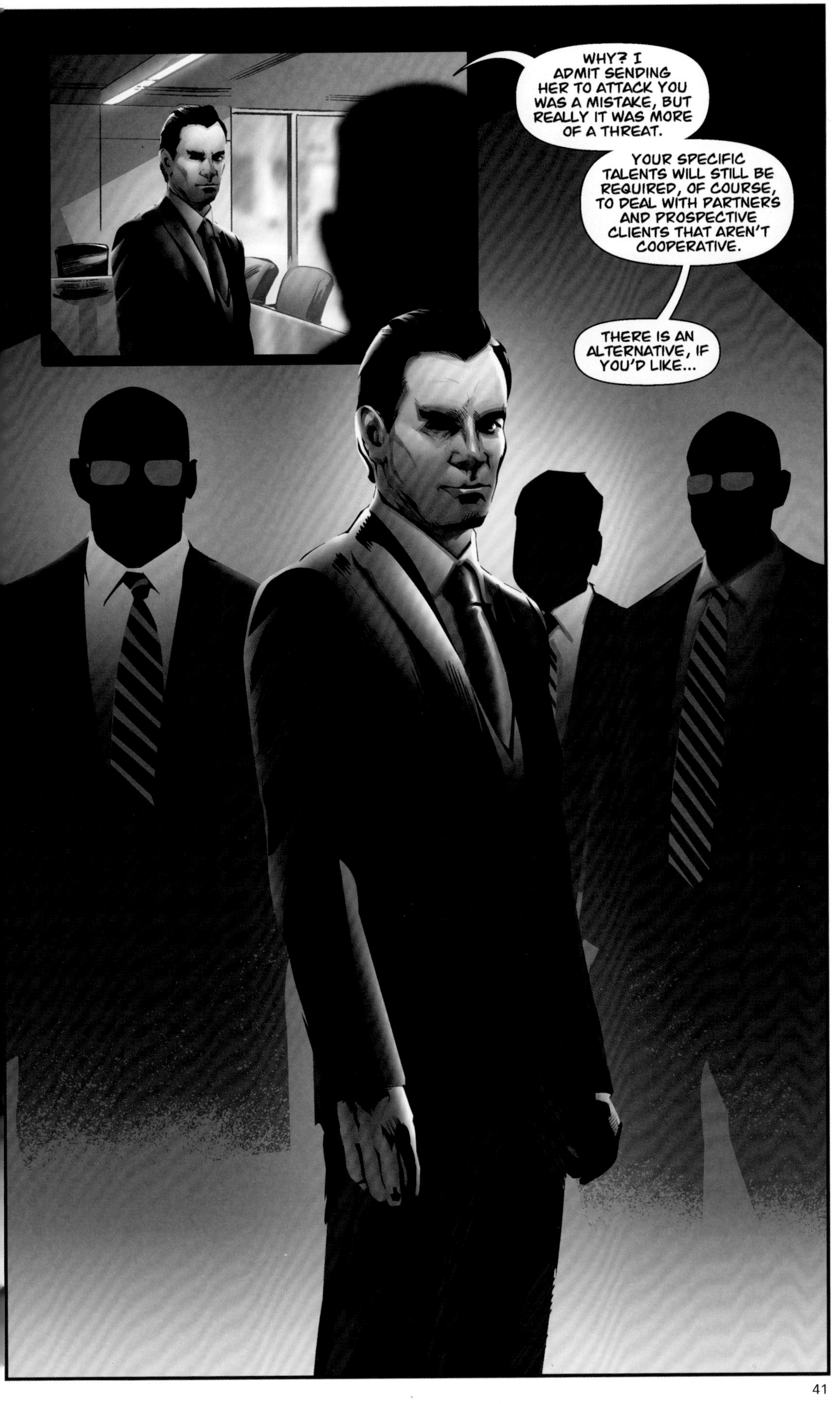
WHY? I ADMIT SENDING HER TO ATTACK YOU WAS A MISTAKE, BUT REALLY IT WAS MORE OF A THREAT.
YOUR SPECIFIC TALENTS WILL STILL BE REQUIRED, OF COURSE, TO DEAL WITH PARTNERS AND PROSPECTIVE CLIENTS THAT AREN'T COOPERATIVE.
THERE IS AN ALTERNATIVE, IF YOU'D LIKE...

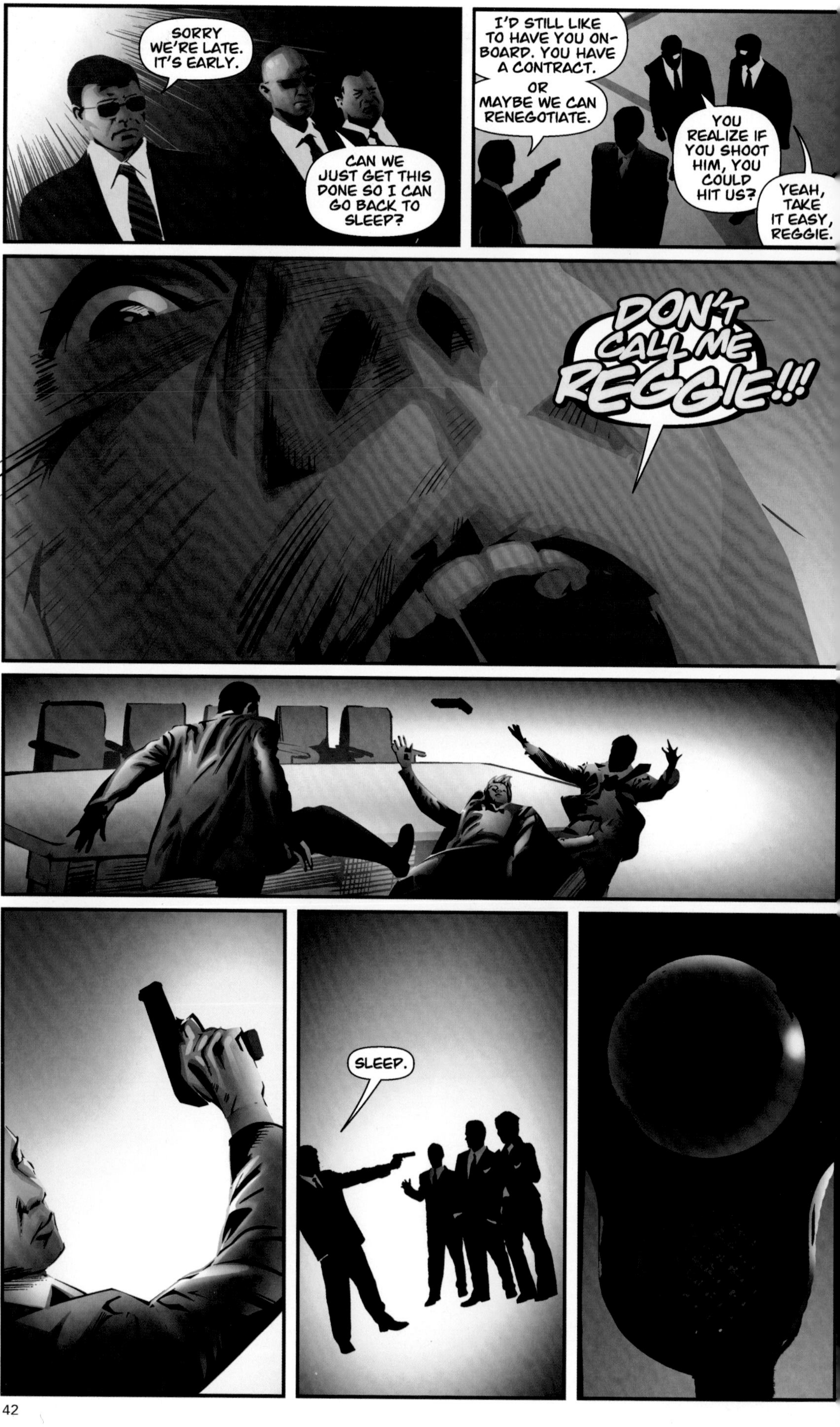
SORRY WE'RE LATE. IT'S EARLY.
CAN WE JUST GET THIS DONE SO I CAN GO BACK TO SLEEP?
I'D STILL LIKE TO HAVE YOU ON-BOARD. YOU HAVE A CONTRACT.
OR MAYBE WE CAN RENEGOTIATE.
YOU REALIZE IF YOU SHOOT HIM, YOU COULD HIT US?
YEAH, TAKE IT EASY, REGGIE.
DON'T CALL ME REGGIE!!!
SLEEP.

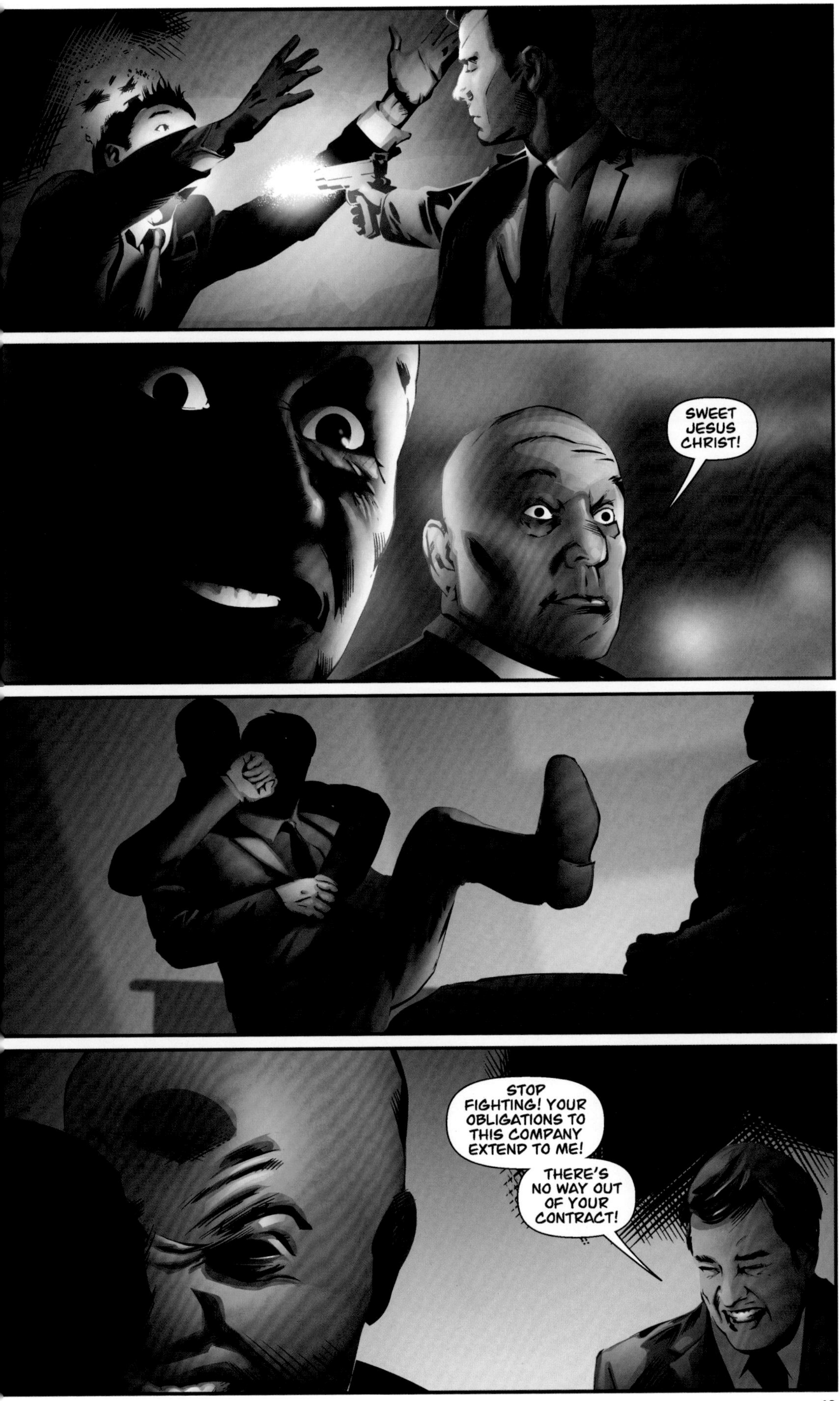
SWEET JESUS CHRIST!
STOP FIGHTING! YOUR OBLIGATIONS TO THIS COMPANY EXTEND TO ME!
THERE'S NO WAY OUT OF YOUR CONTRACT!

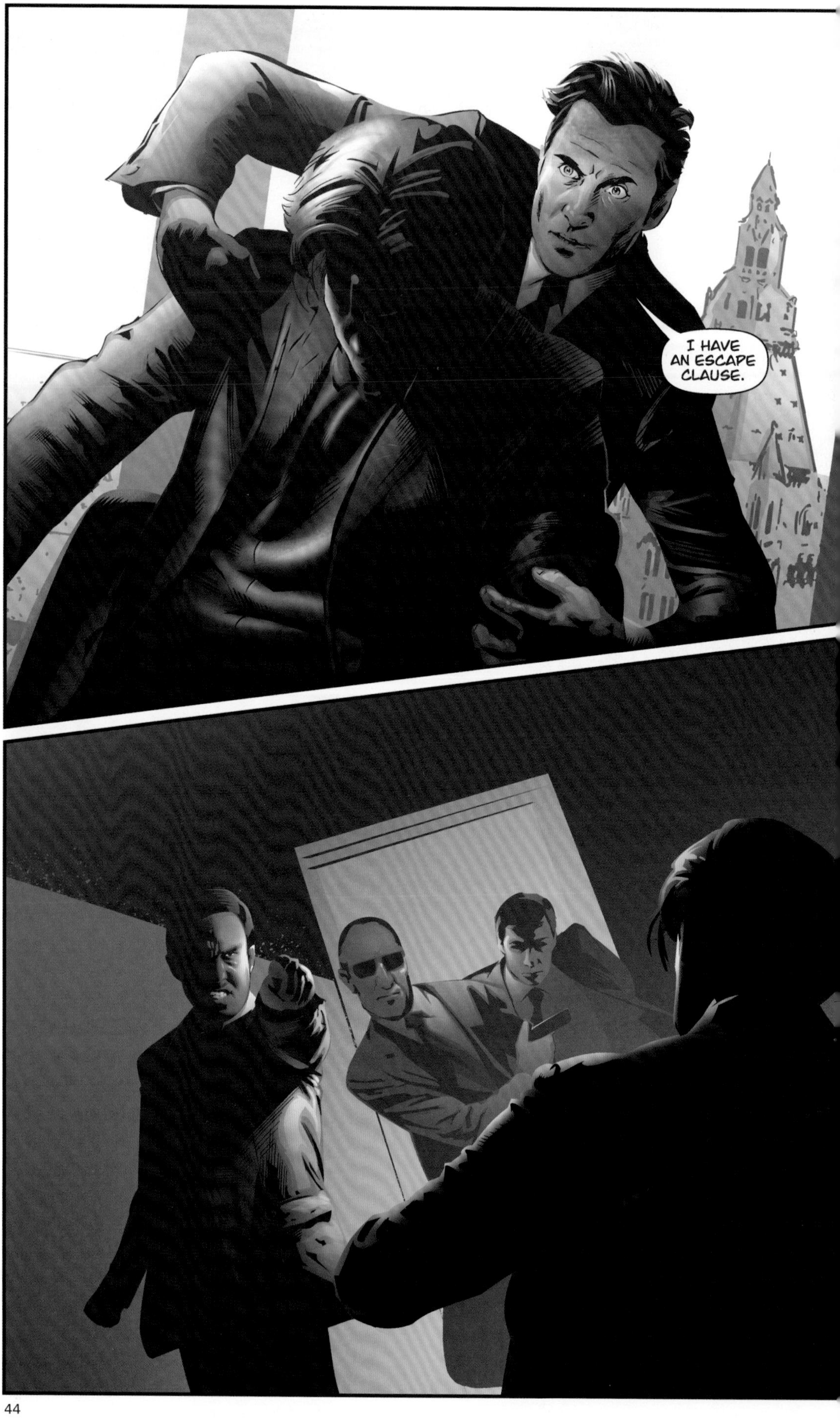
I HAVE AN ESCAPE CLAUSE.

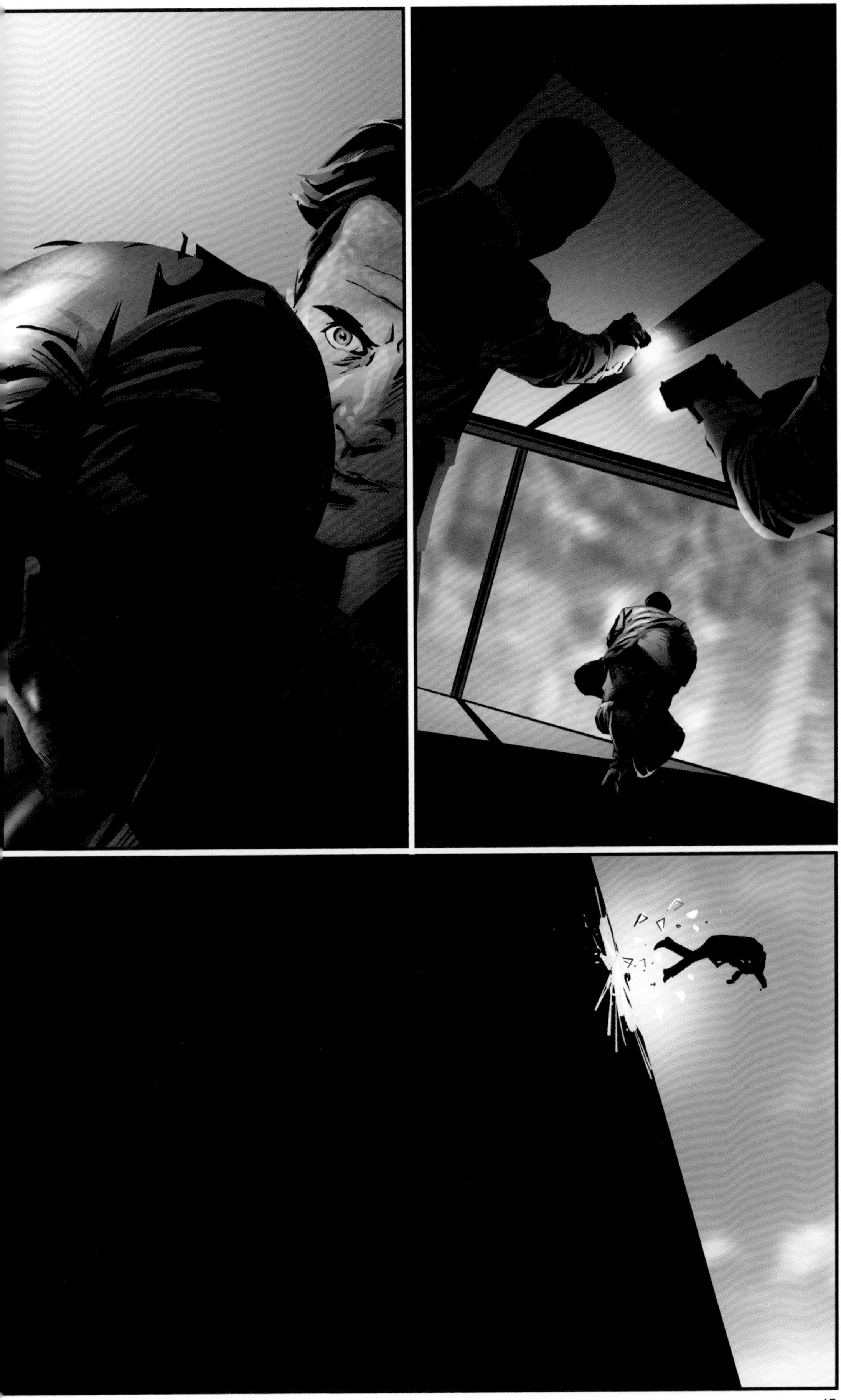

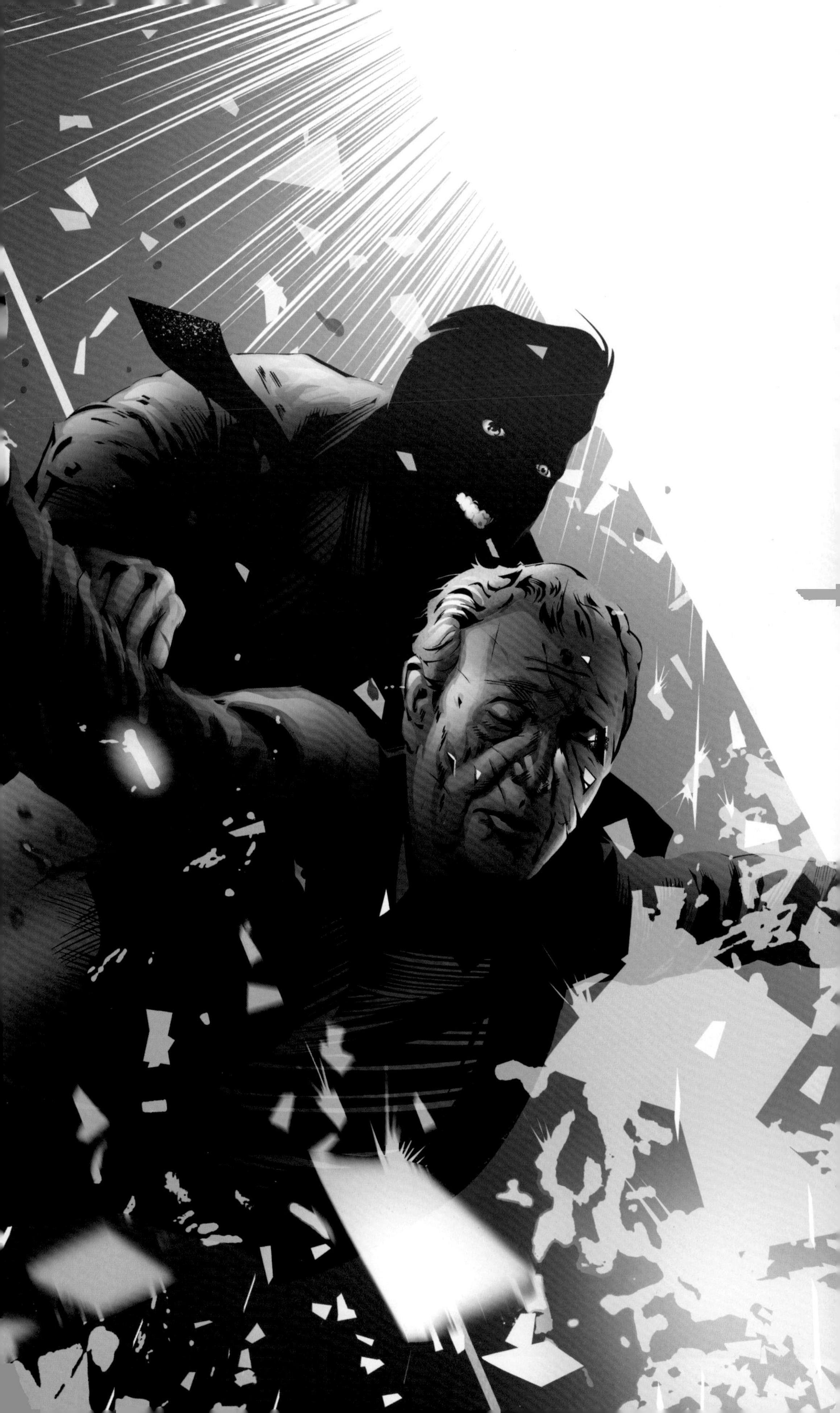

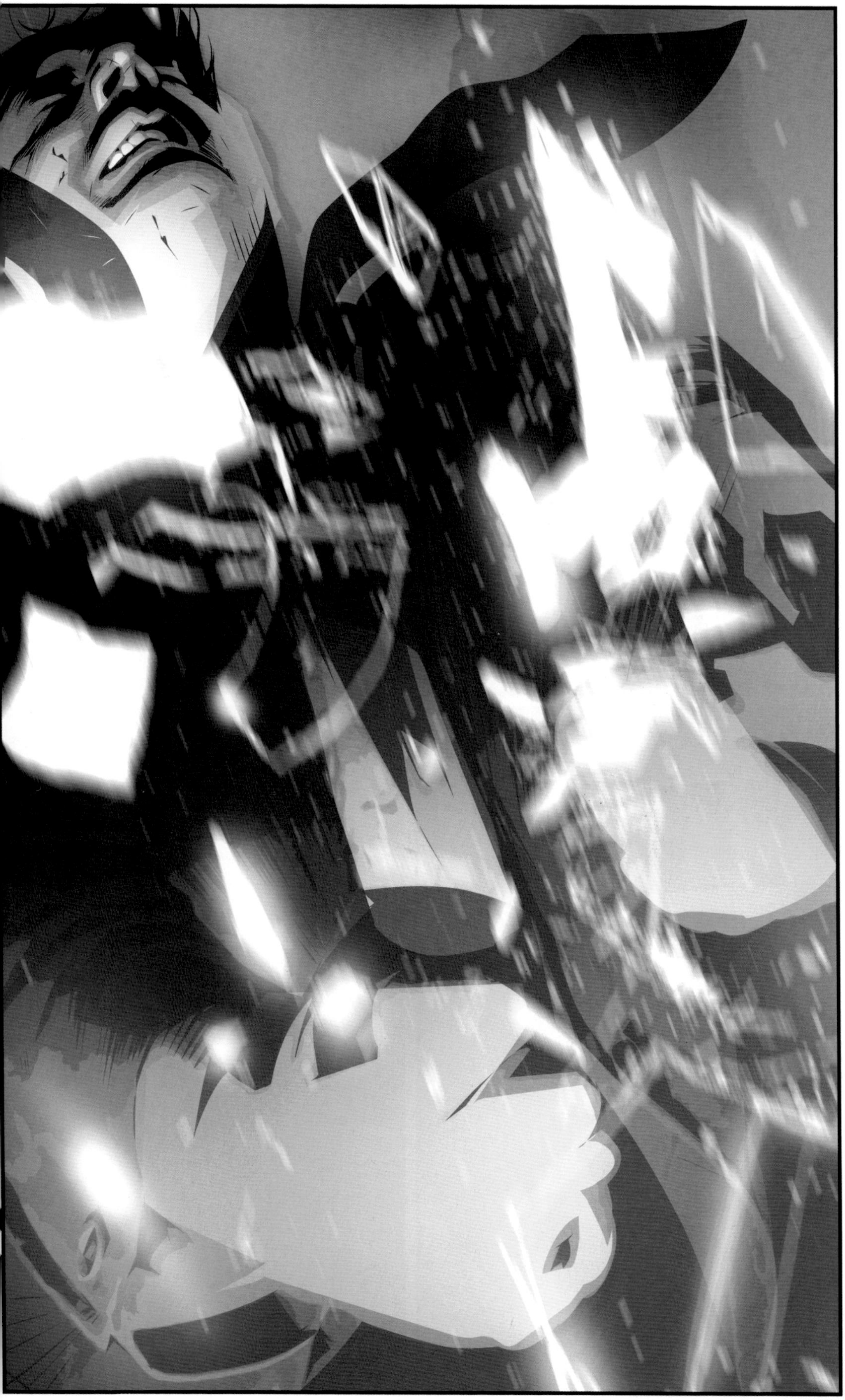

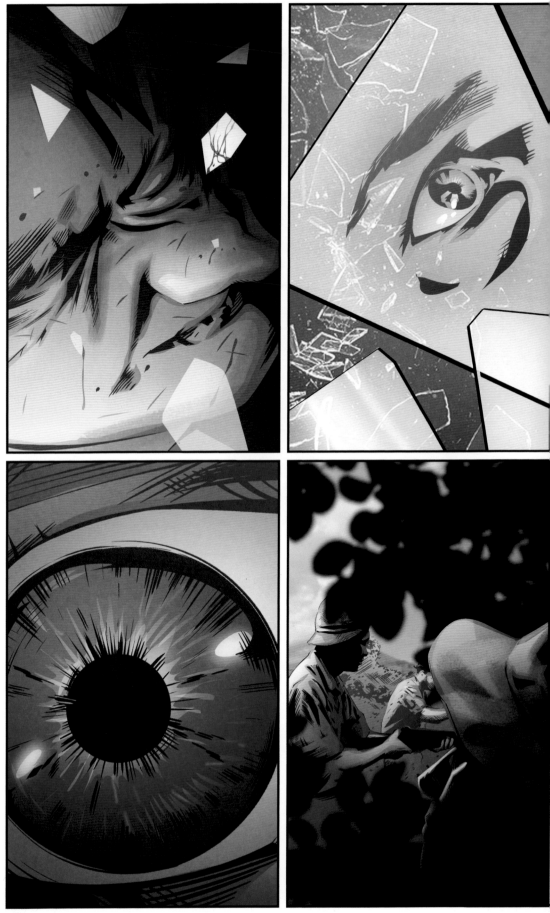

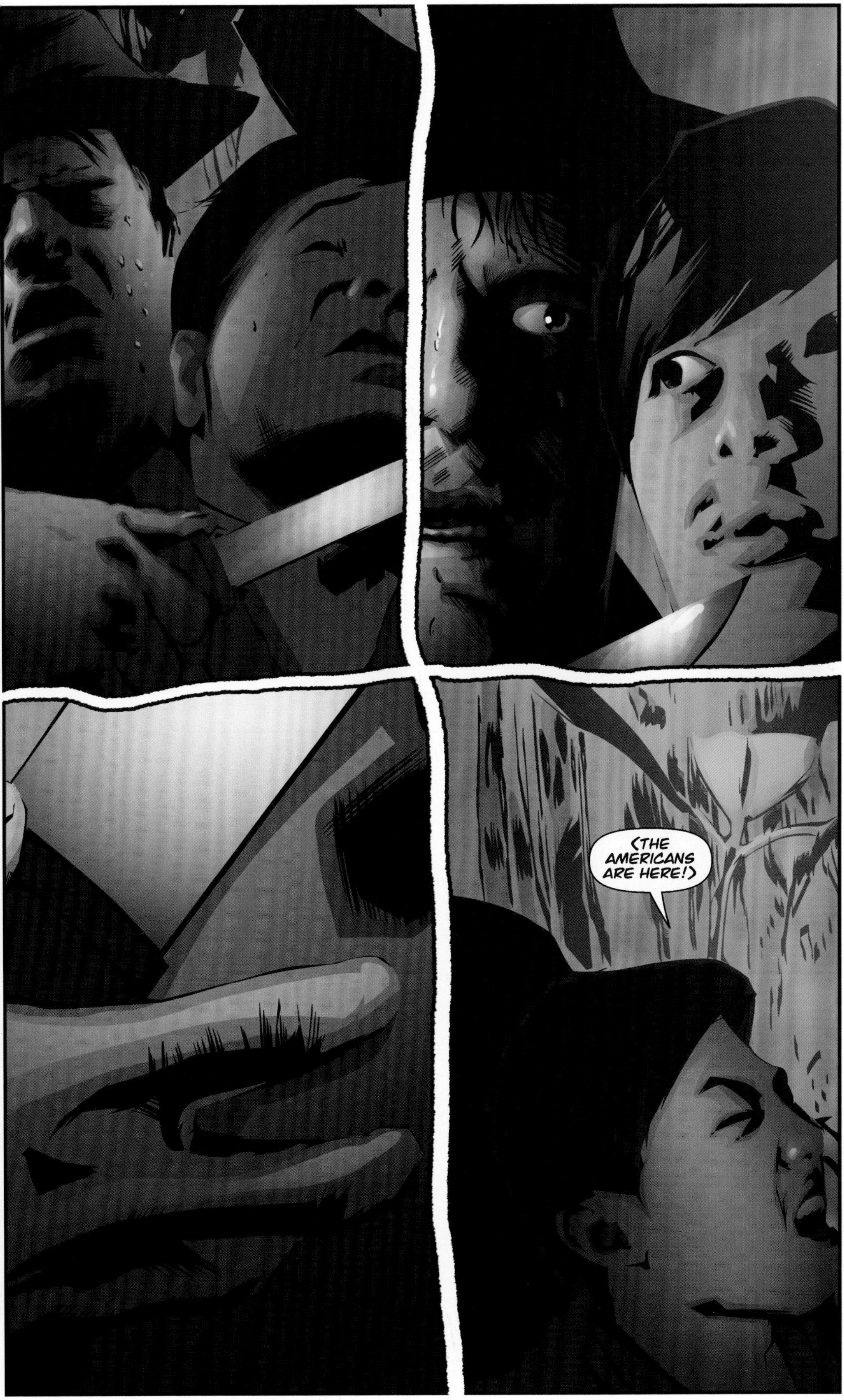
<THE AMERICANS ARE HERE!>

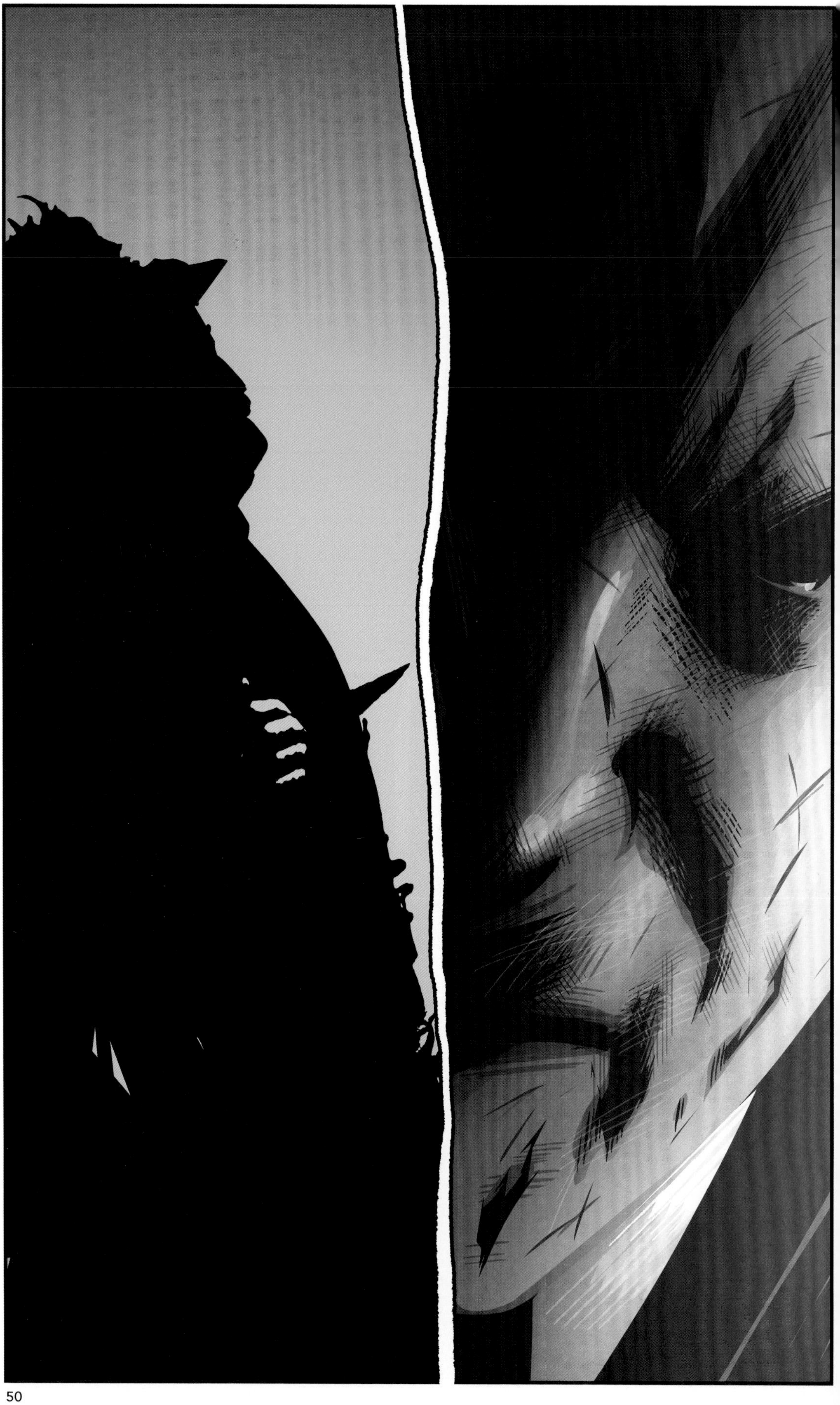

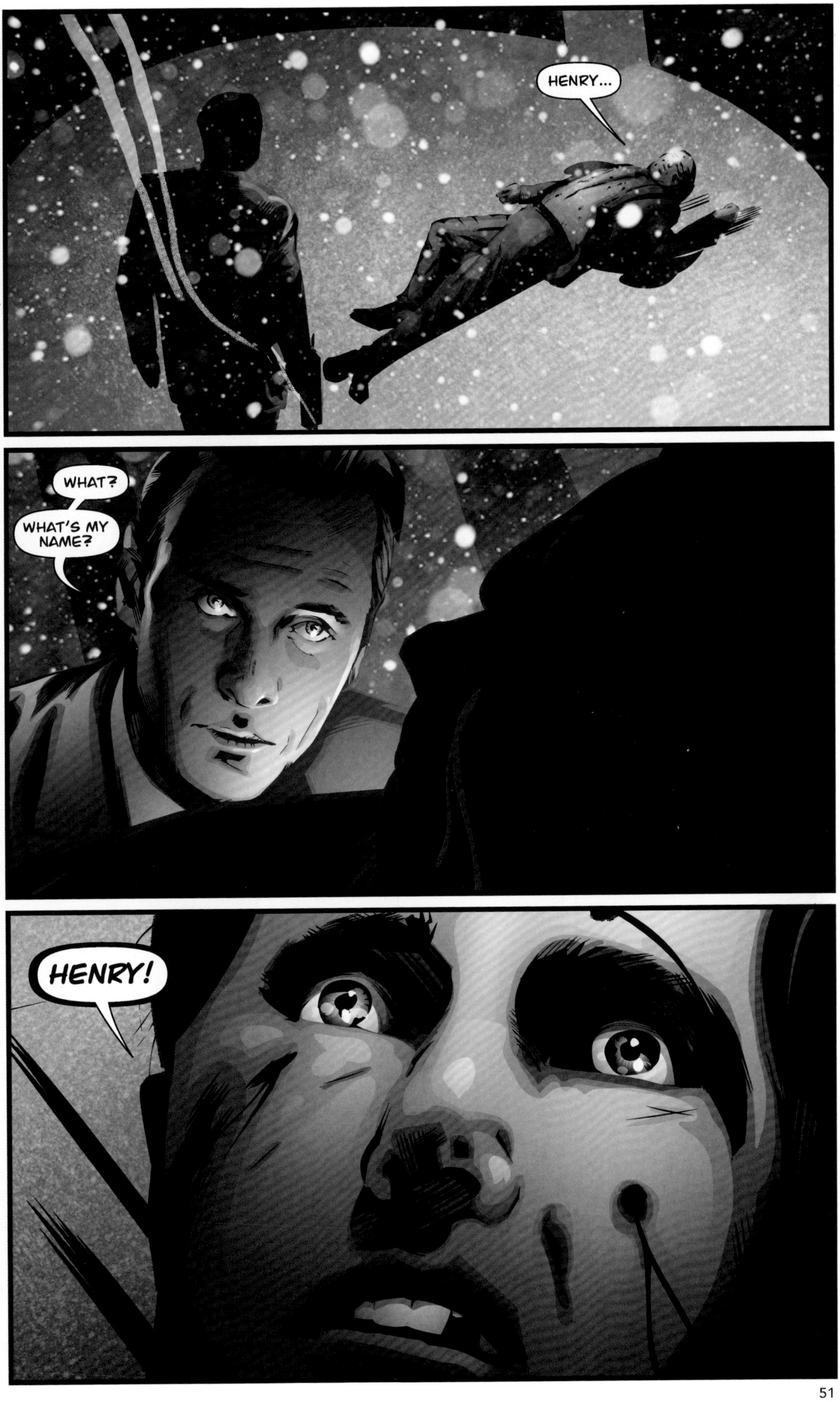
HENRY...
WHAT?
WHAT'S MY NAME?
HENRY!

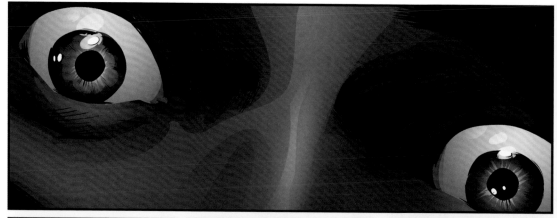

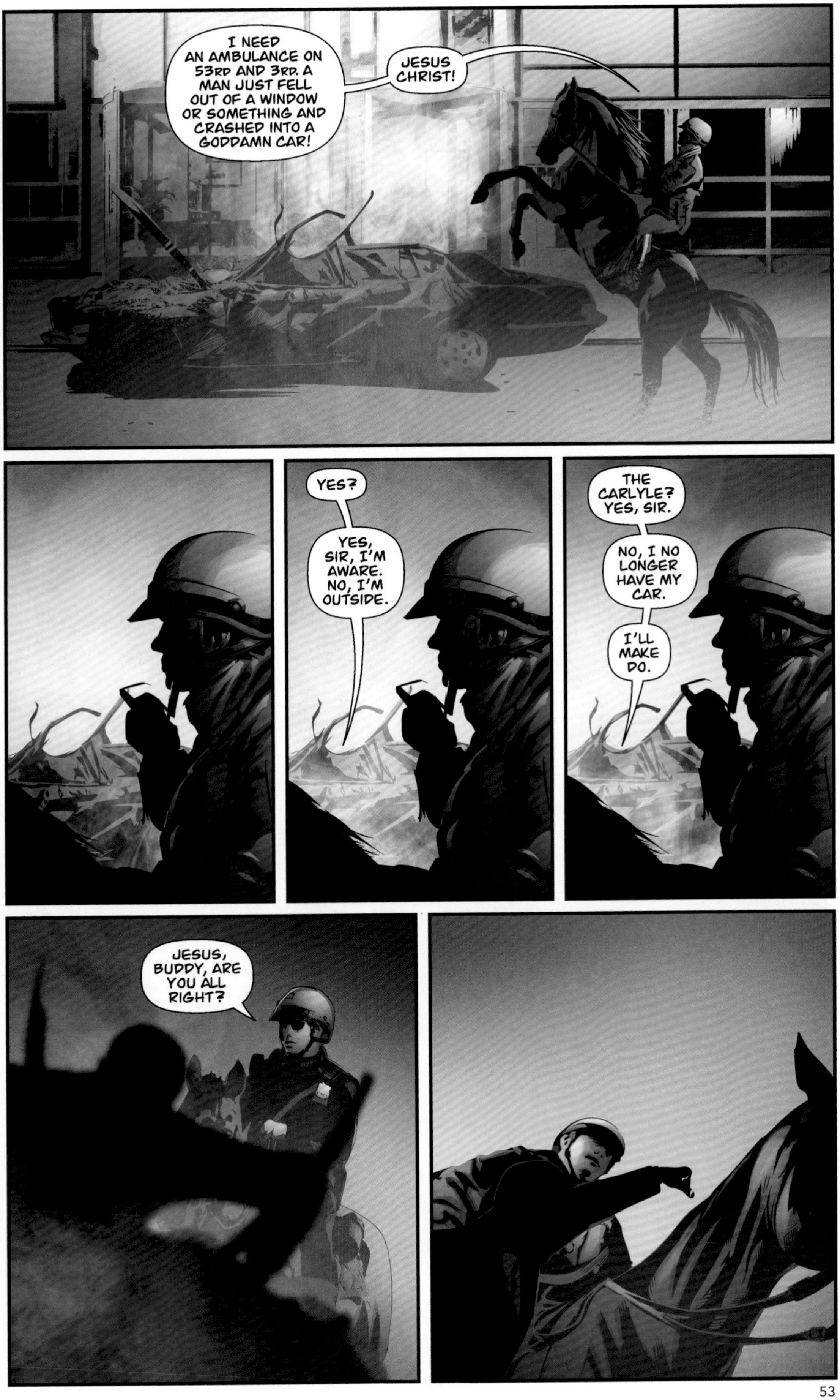
I NEED AN AMBULANCE ON 53RD AND 3RD. A MAN JUST FELL OUT OF A WINDOW OR SOMETHING AND CRASHED INTO A GODDAMN CAR!
JESUS CHRIST!
YES?
YES, SIR, I'M AWARE. NO, I'M OUTSIDE.
THE CARLYLE? YES, SIR.
NO, I NO LONGER HAVE MY CAR.
I'LL MAKE DO.
JESUS, BUDDY, ARE YOU ALL RIGHT?

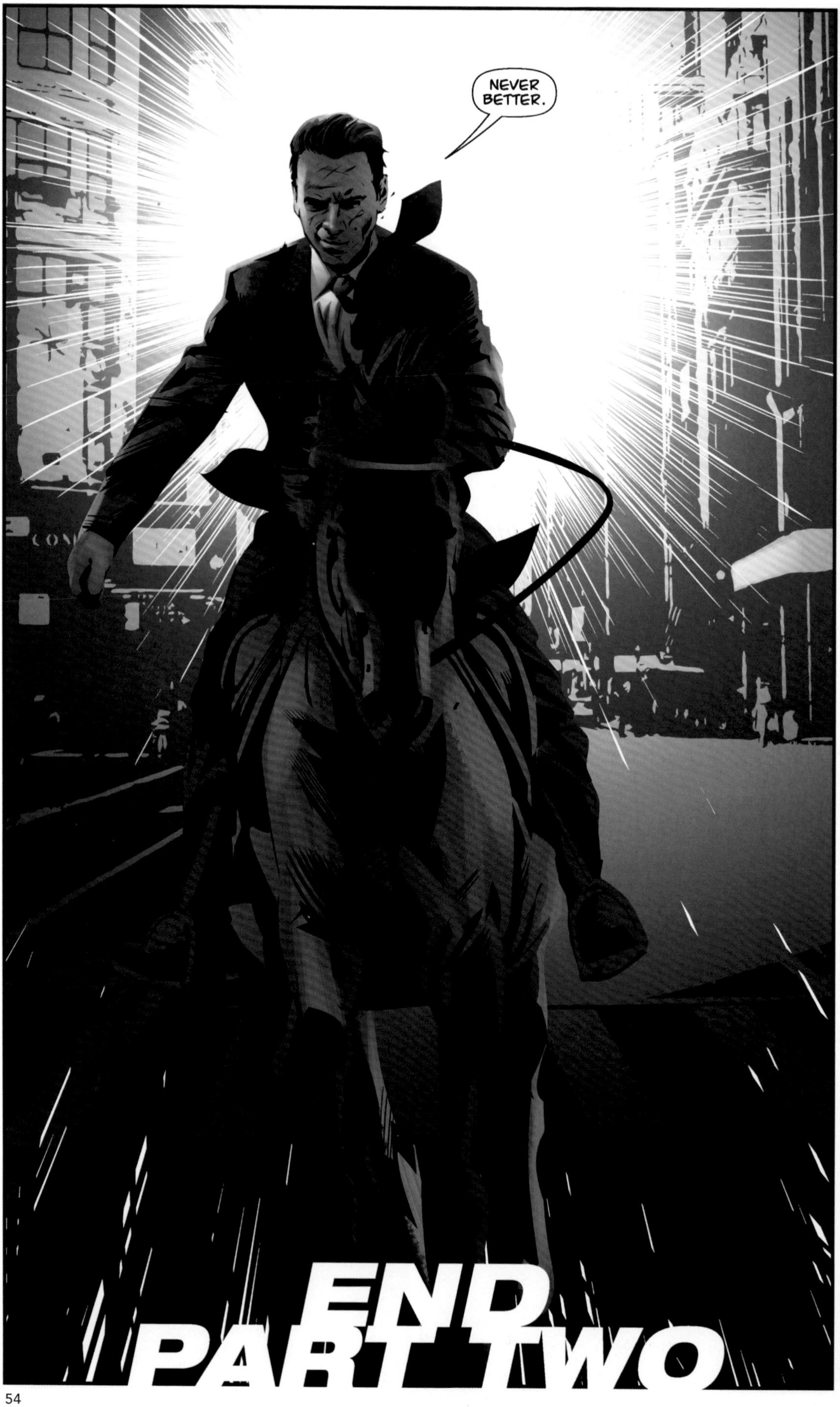
NEVER BETTER.
END
PART TWO

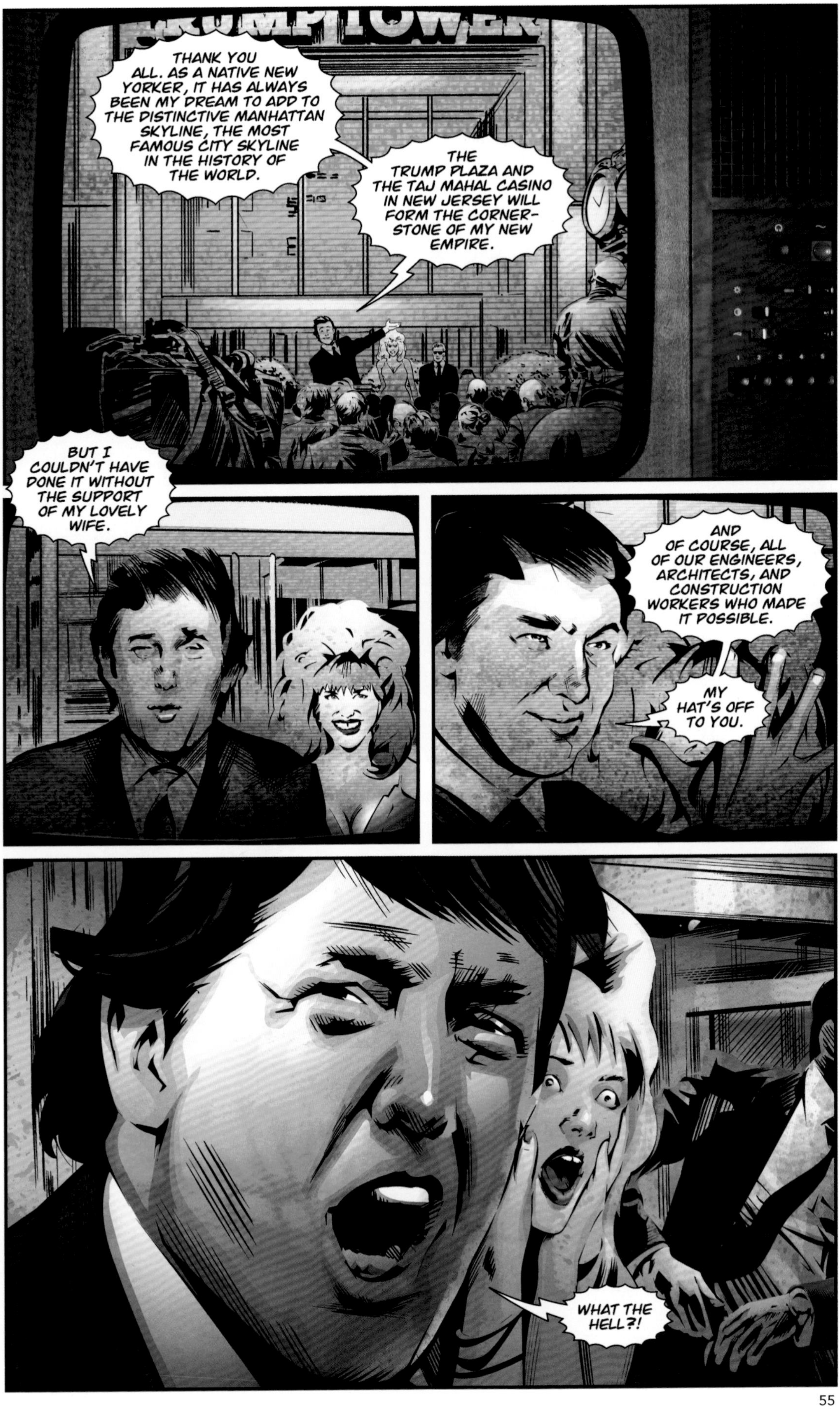
TRUMP TOWER
THANK YOU ALL. AS A NATIVE NEW YORKER, IT HAS ALWAYS BEEN MY DREAM TO ADD TO THE DISTINCTIVE MANHATTAN SKYLINE, THE MOST FAMOUS CITY SKYLINE IN THE HISTORY OF THE WORLD.
THE TRUMP PLAZA AND THE TAJ MAHAL CASINO IN NEW JERSEY WILL FORM THE CORNER-STONE OF MY NEW EMPIRE.
BUT I COULDN'T HAVE DONE IT WITHOUT THE SUPPORT OF MY LOVELY WIFE.
AND OF COURSE, ALL OF OUR ENGINEERS, ARCHITECTS, AND CONSTRUCTION WORKERS WHO MADE IT POSSIBLE.
MY HAT'S OFF TO YOU.
WHAT THE HELL?!

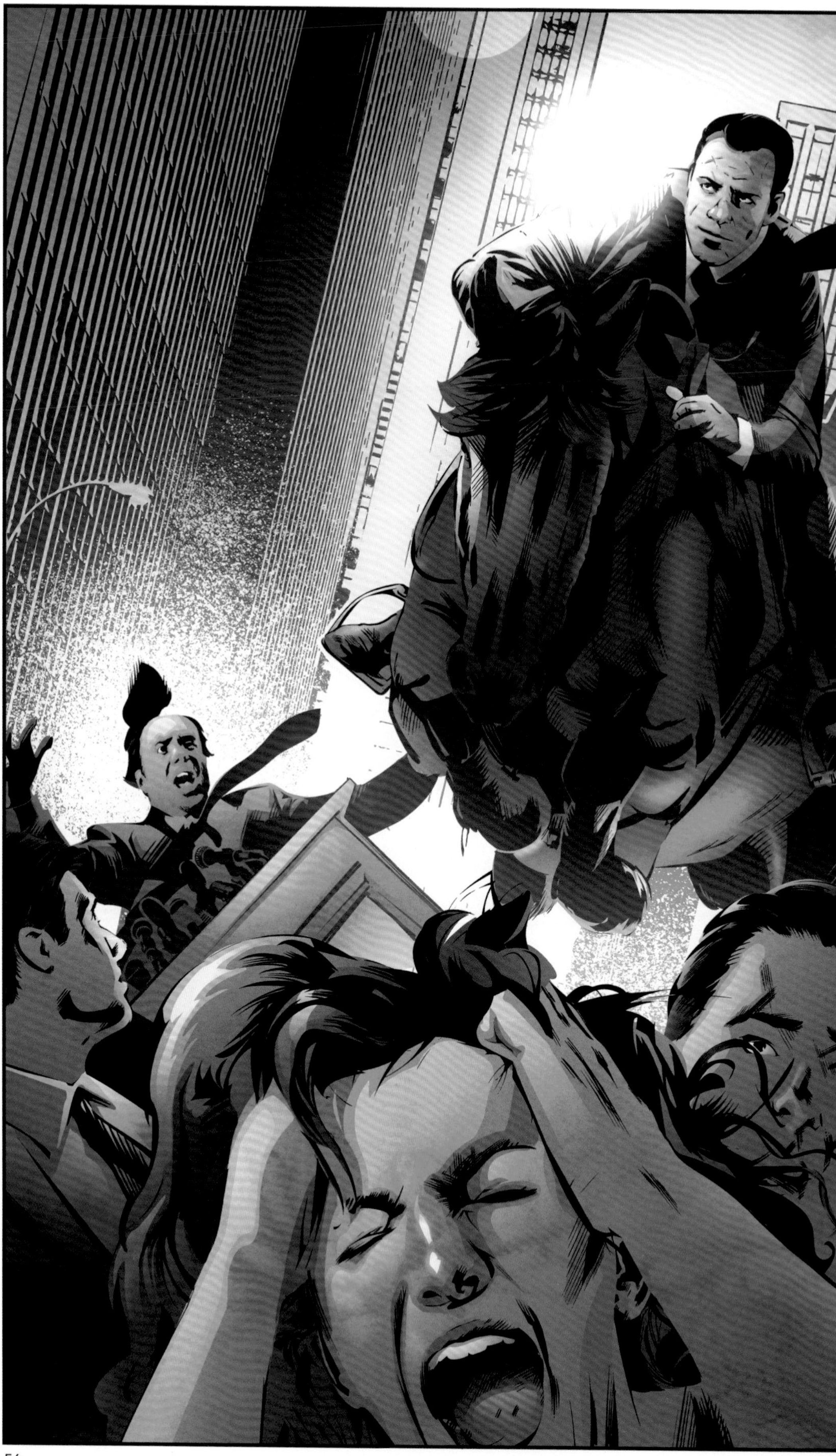

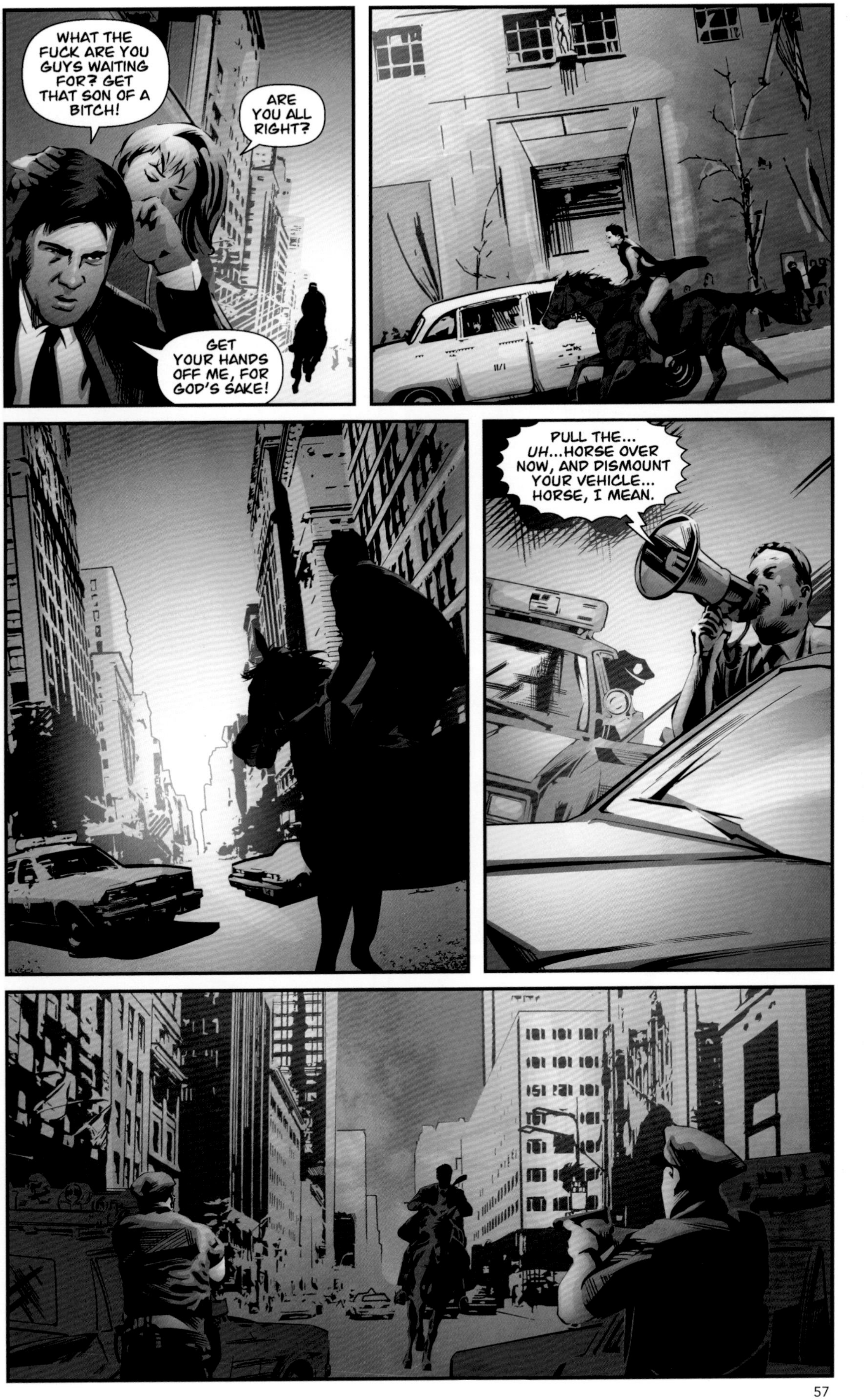

WHAT THE FUCK ARE YOU GUYS WAITING FOR? GET THAT SON OF A BITCH!
ARE YOU ALL RIGHT?
GET YOUR HANDS OFF ME, FOR GOD'S SAKE!
PULL THE... UH...HORSE OVER NOW, AND DISMOUNT YOUR VEHICLE... HORSE, I MEAN.

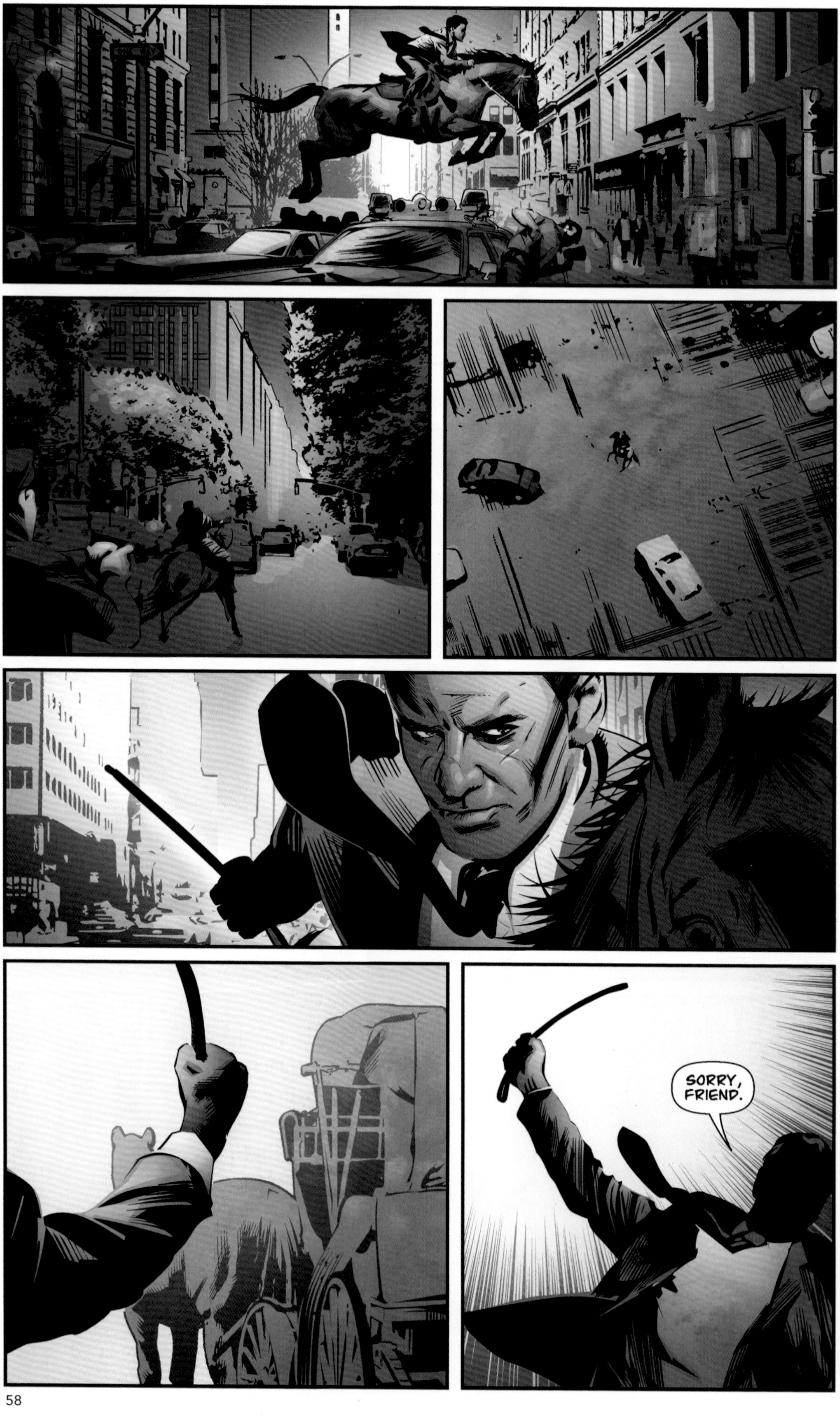
SORRY, FRIEND.

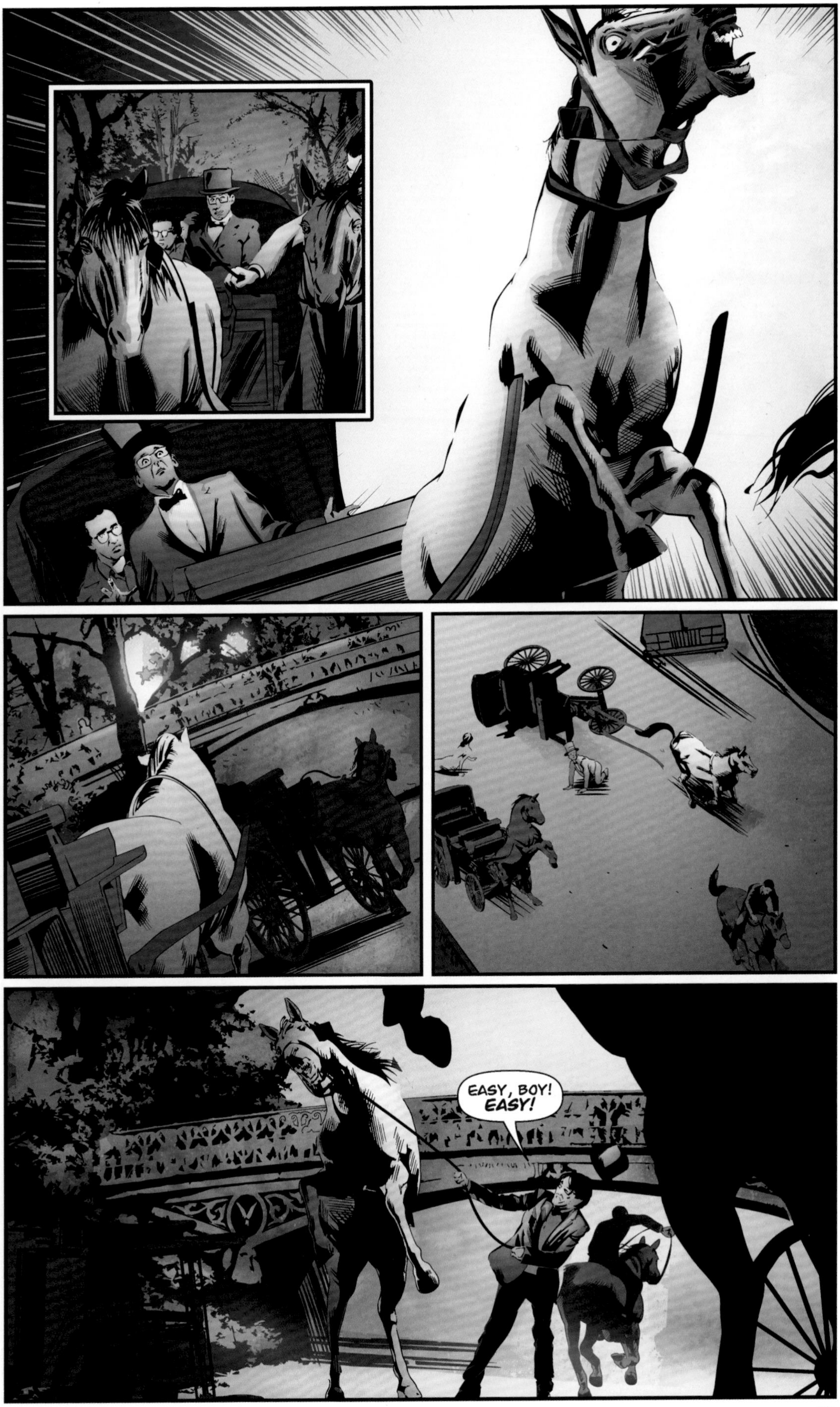
EASY, BOY! EASY!

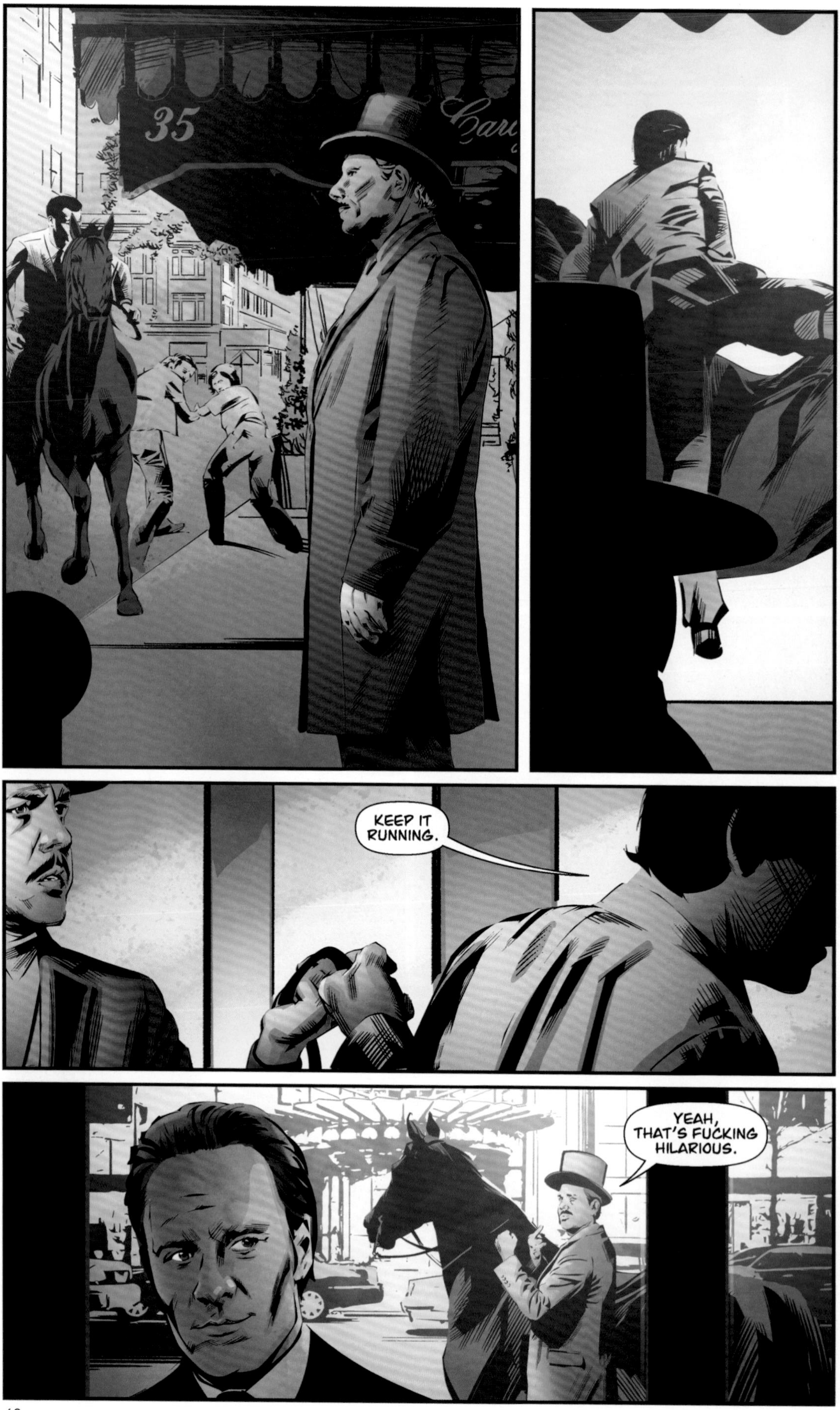
35
KEEP IT RUNNING.
YEAH, THAT'S FUCKING HILARIOUS.

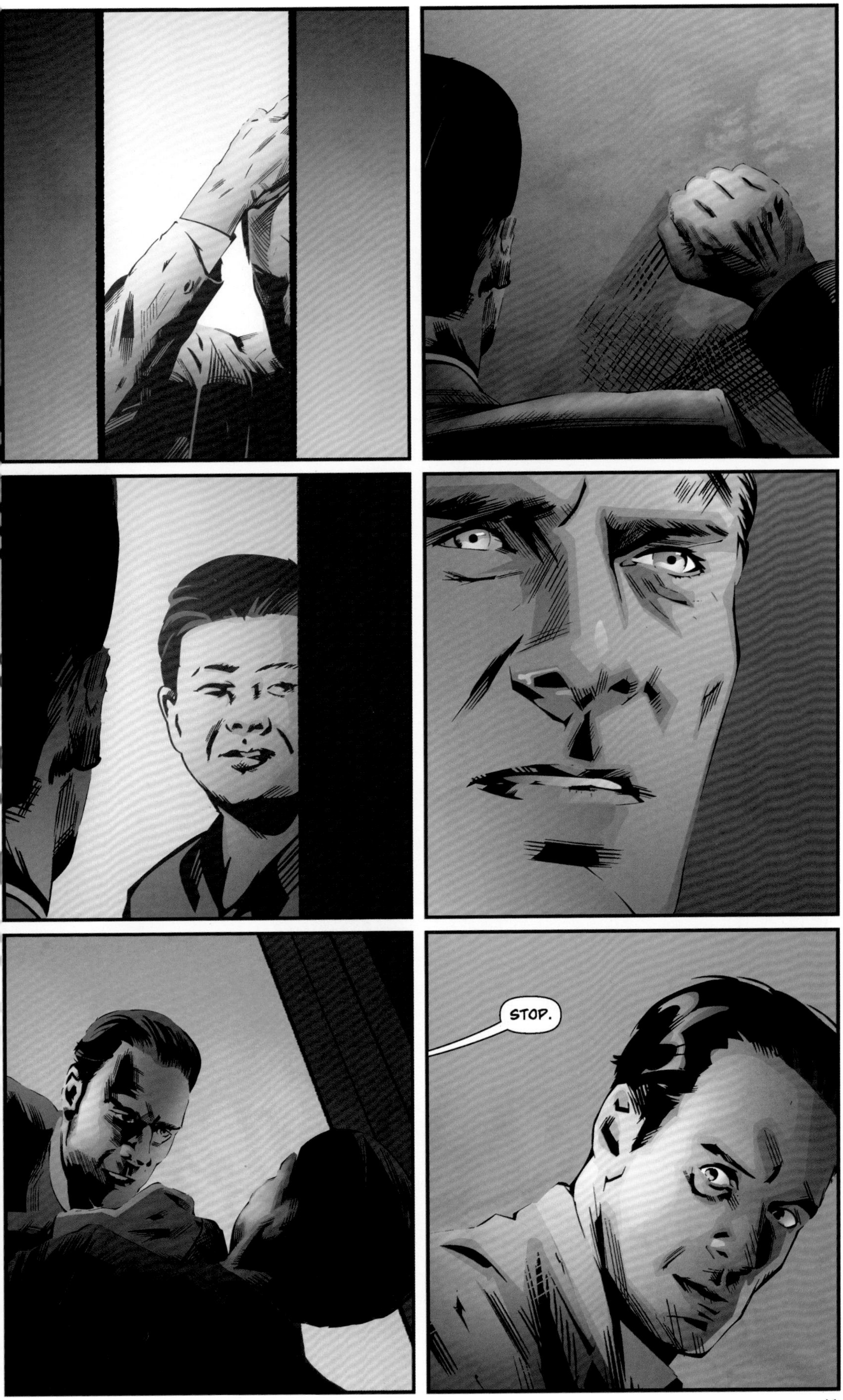
STOP.

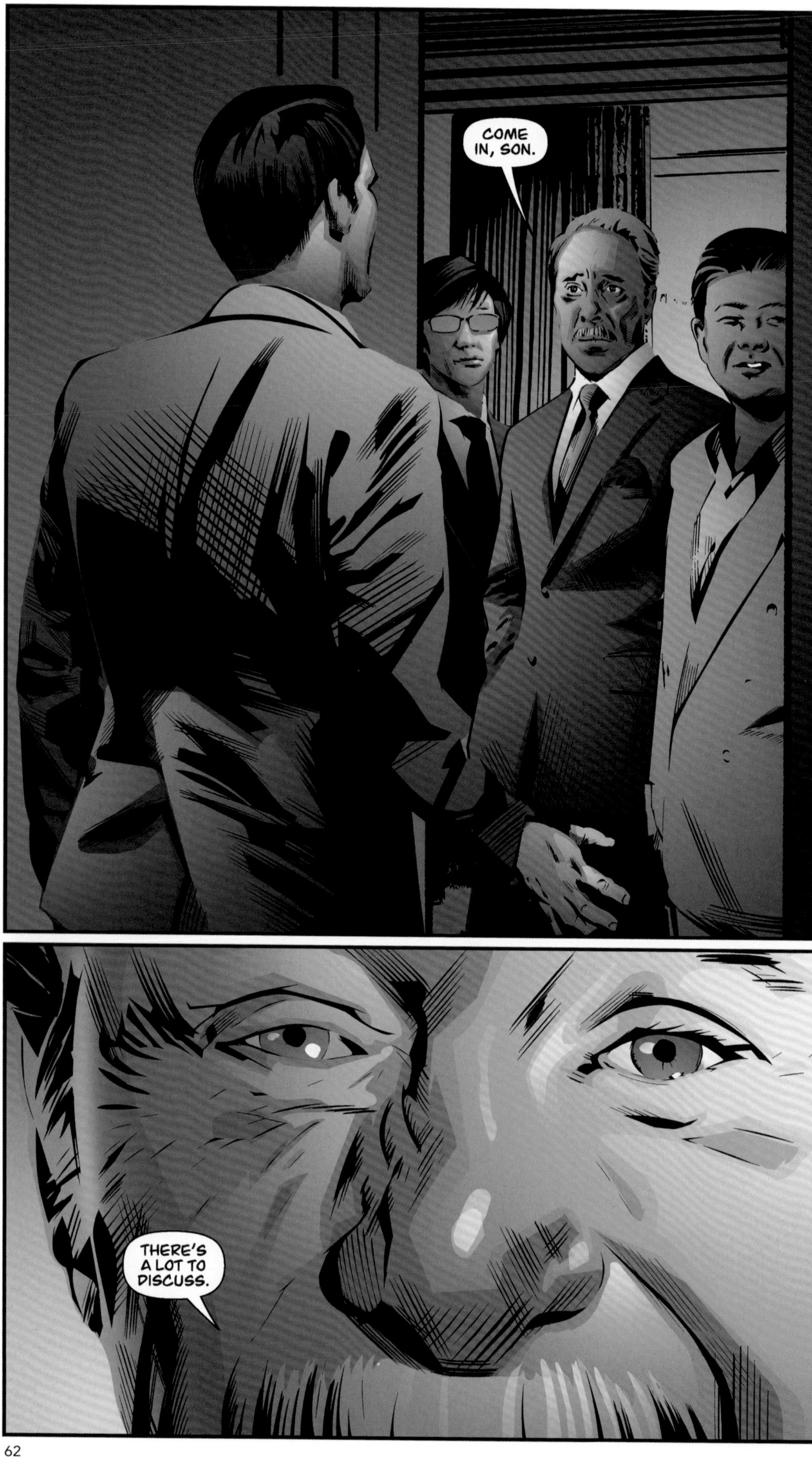
COME IN, SON.
THERE'S A LOT TO DISCUSS.

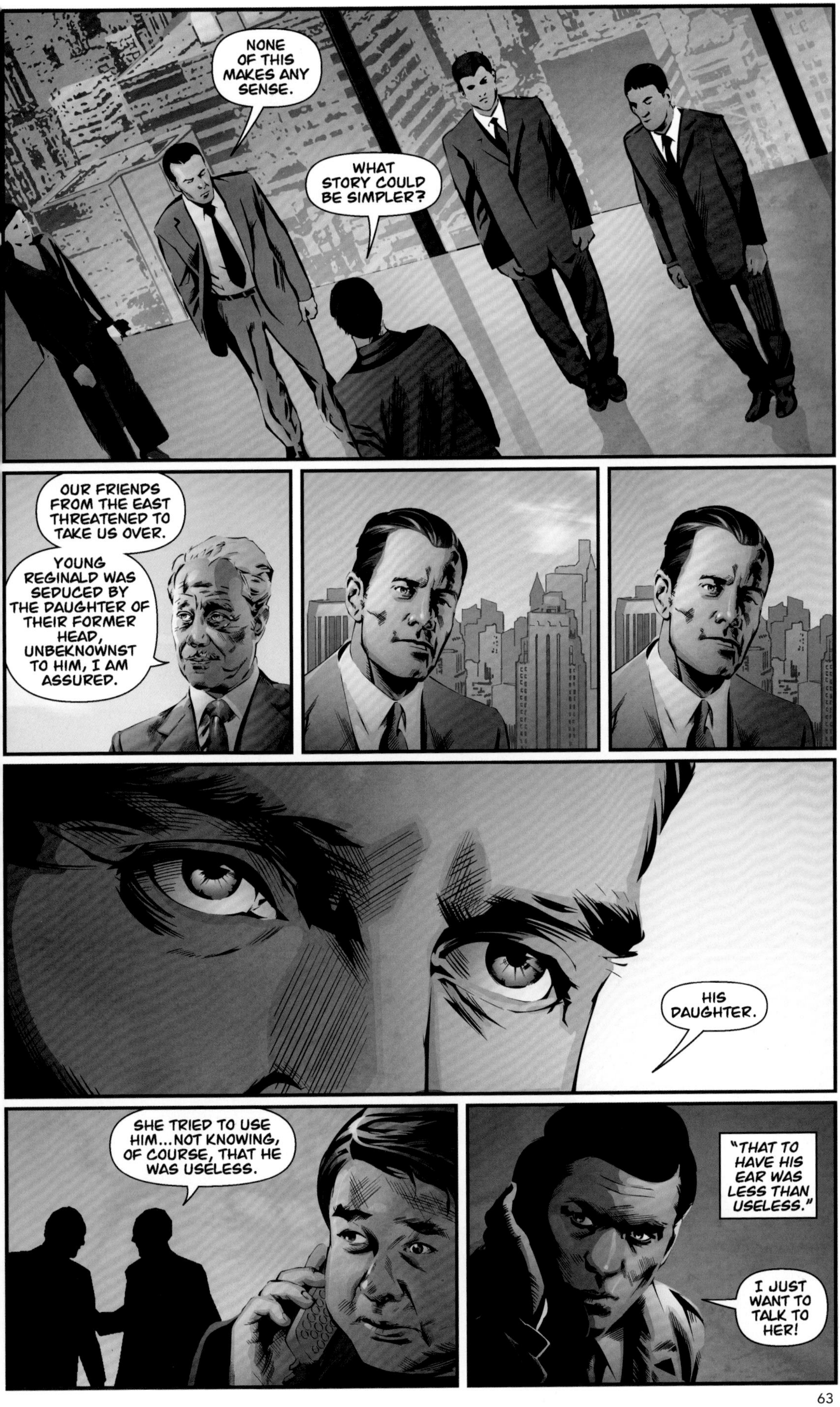
NONE OF THIS MAKES ANY SENSE.
WHAT STORY COULD BE SIMPLER?
OUR FRIENDS FROM THE EAST THREATENED TO TAKE US OVER.
YOUNG REGINALD WAS SEDUCED BY THE DAUGHTER OF THEIR FORMER HEAD, UNBEKNOWNST TO HIM, I AM ASSURED.
HIS DAUGHTER.
SHE TRIED TO USE HIM...NOT KNOWING, OF COURSE, THAT HE WAS USELESS.
"THAT TO HAVE HIS EAR WAS LESS THAN USELESS."
I JUST WANT TO TALK TO HER!

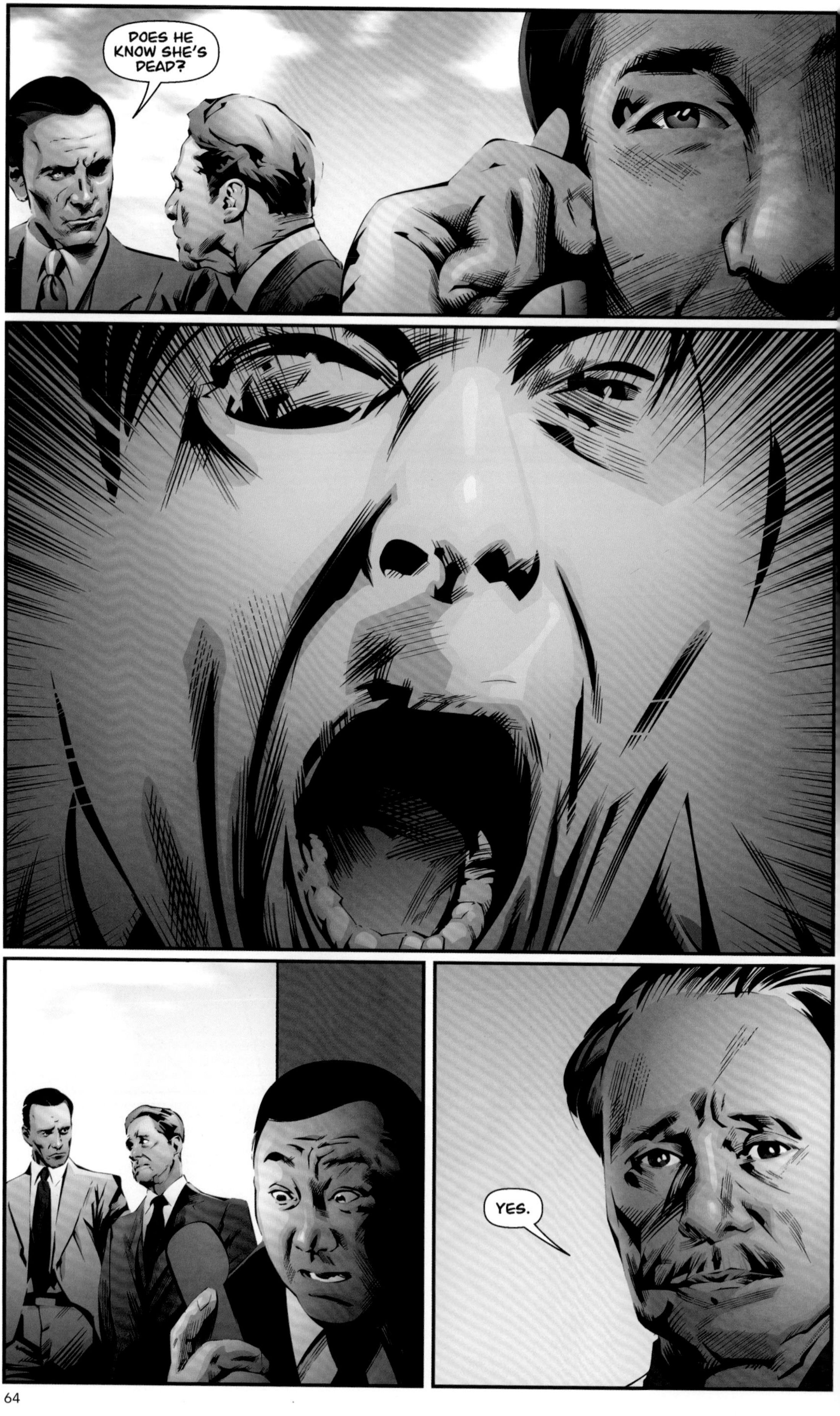

DOES HE KNOW SHE'S DEAD?
YES.

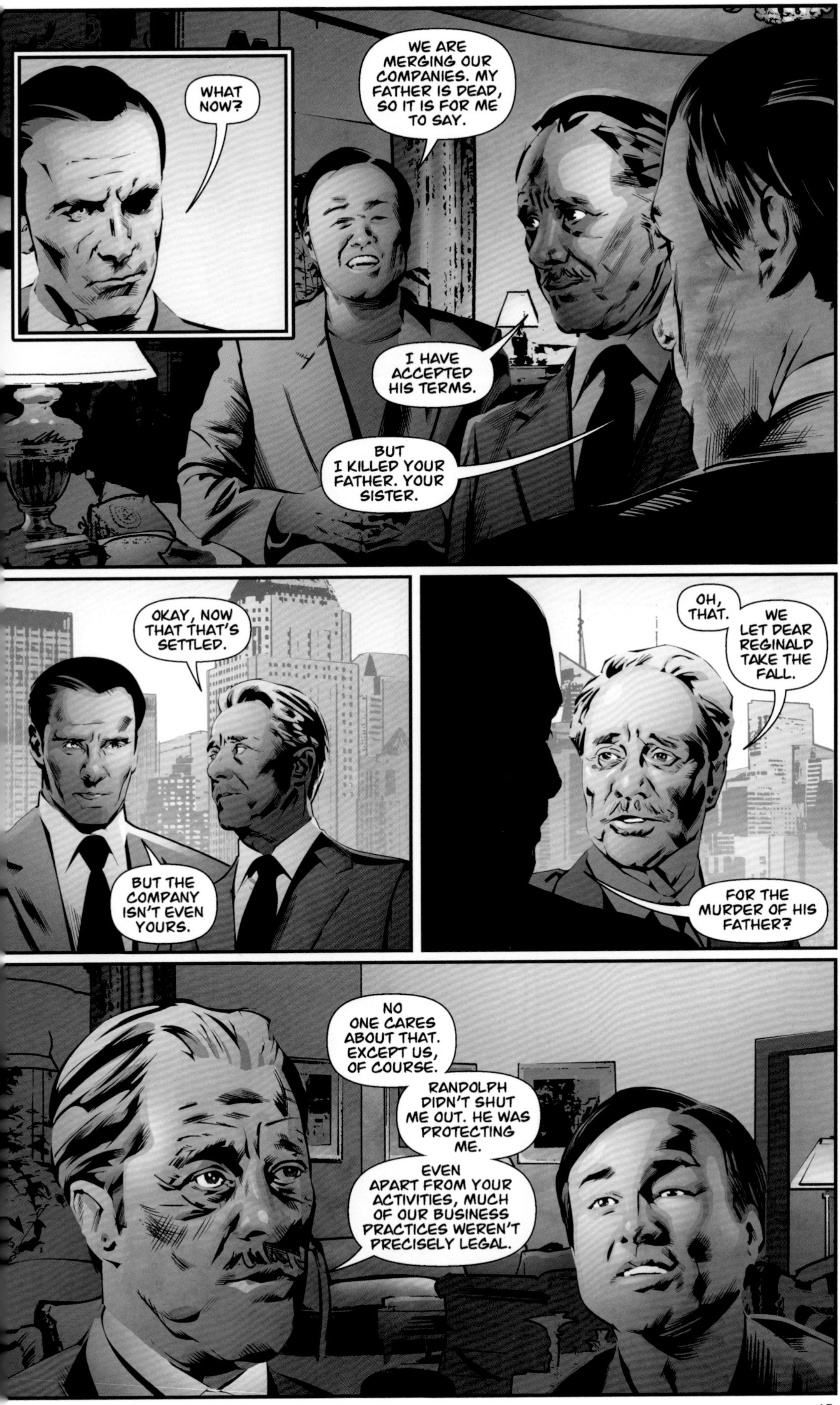
WHAT NOW?
WE ARE MERGING OUR COMPANIES. MY FATHER IS DEAD, SO IT IS FOR ME TO SAY.
I HAVE ACCEPTED HIS TERMS.
BUT I KILLED YOUR FATHER. YOUR SISTER.
OKAY, NOW THAT THAT'S SETTLED.
BUT THE COMPANY ISN'T EVEN YOURS.
OH, THAT.
WE LET DEAR REGINALD TAKE THE FALL.
FOR THE MURDER OF HIS FATHER?
NO ONE CARES ABOUT THAT. EXCEPT US, OF COURSE.
RANDOLPH DIDN'T SHUT ME OUT. HE WAS PROTECTING ME.
EVEN APART FROM YOUR ACTIVITIES, MUCH OF OUR BUSINESS PRACTICES WEREN'T PRECISELY LEGAL.

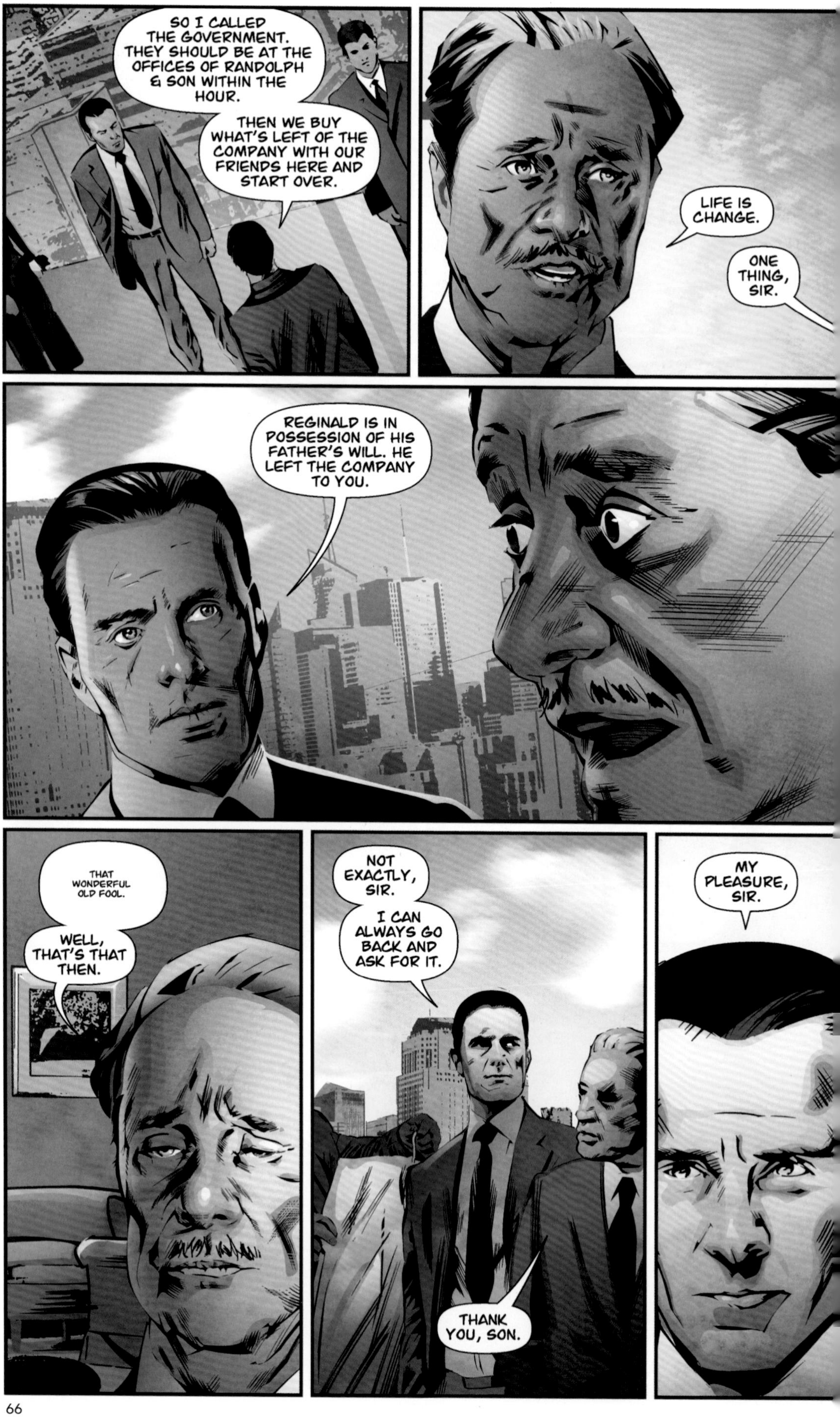

SO I CALLED THE GOVERNMENT. THEY SHOULD BE AT THE OFFICES OF RANDOLPH & SON WITHIN THE HOUR.
THEN WE BUY WHAT'S LEFT OF THE COMPANY WITH OUR FRIENDS HERE AND START OVER.
LIFE IS CHANGE.
ONE THING, SIR.
REGINALD IS IN POSSESSION OF HIS FATHER'S WILL. HE LEFT THE COMPANY TO YOU.
THAT WONDERFUL OLD FOOL.
WELL, THAT'S THAT THEN.
NOT EXACTLY, SIR.
I CAN ALWAYS GO BACK AND ASK FOR IT.
THANK YOU, SON.
MY PLEASURE, SIR.

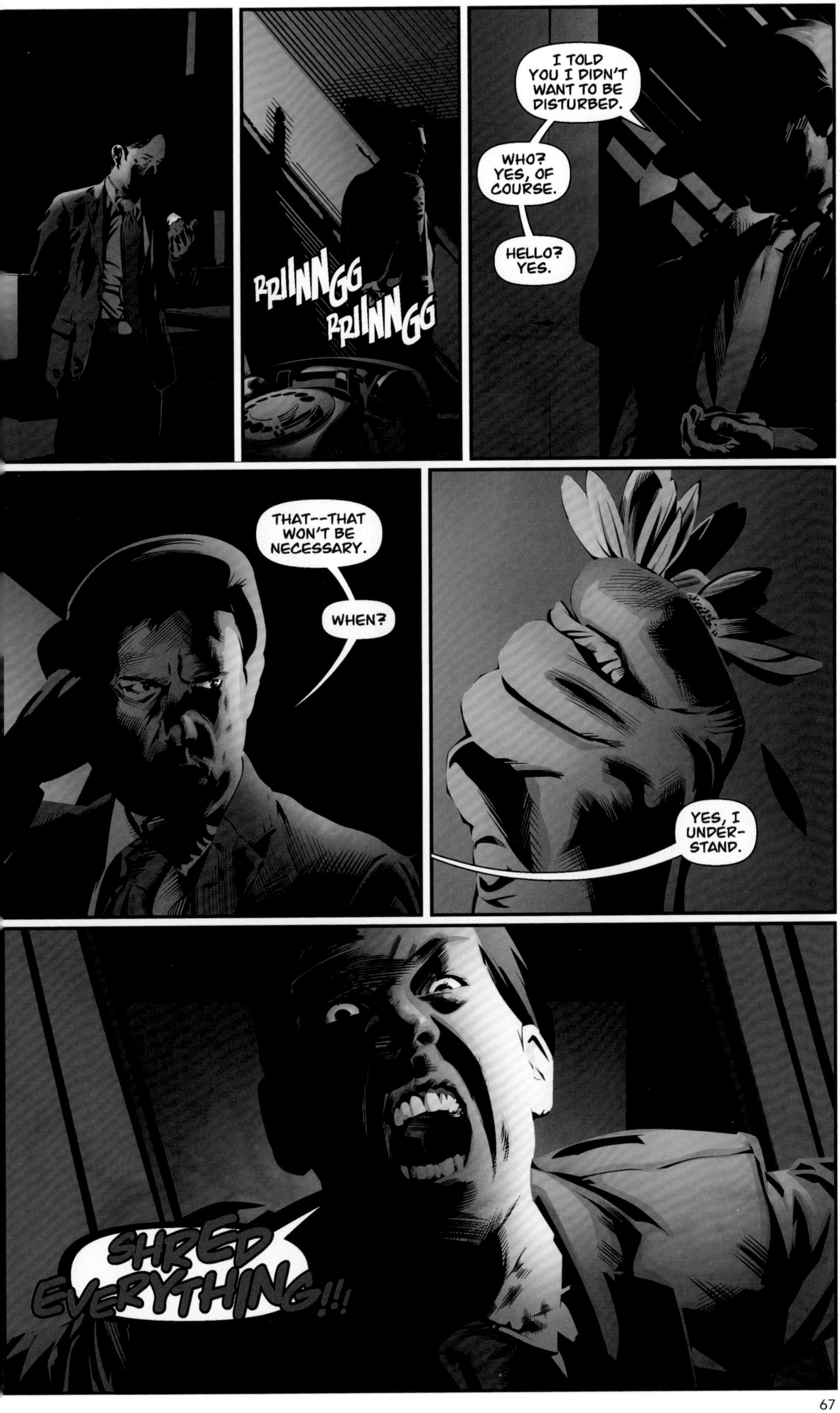

RRIINNGG RRIINNGG
HELLO? YES.
WHO? YES, OF COURSE.
I TOLD YOU I DIDN'T WANT TO BE DISTURBED.
THAT--THAT WON'T BE NECESSARY.
WHEN?
YES, I UNDER-STAND.
SHRED EVERYTHING!!!

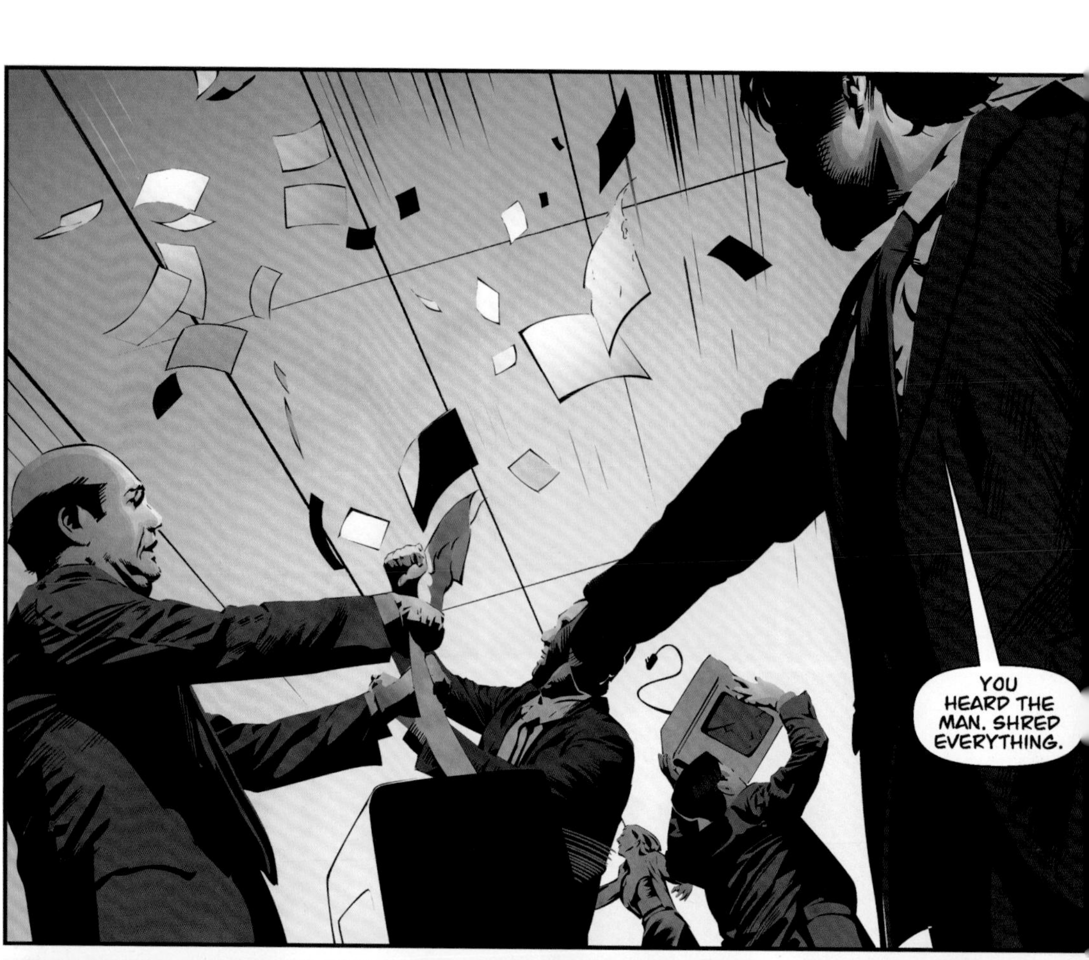
YOU HEARD THE MAN. SHRED EVERYTHING.

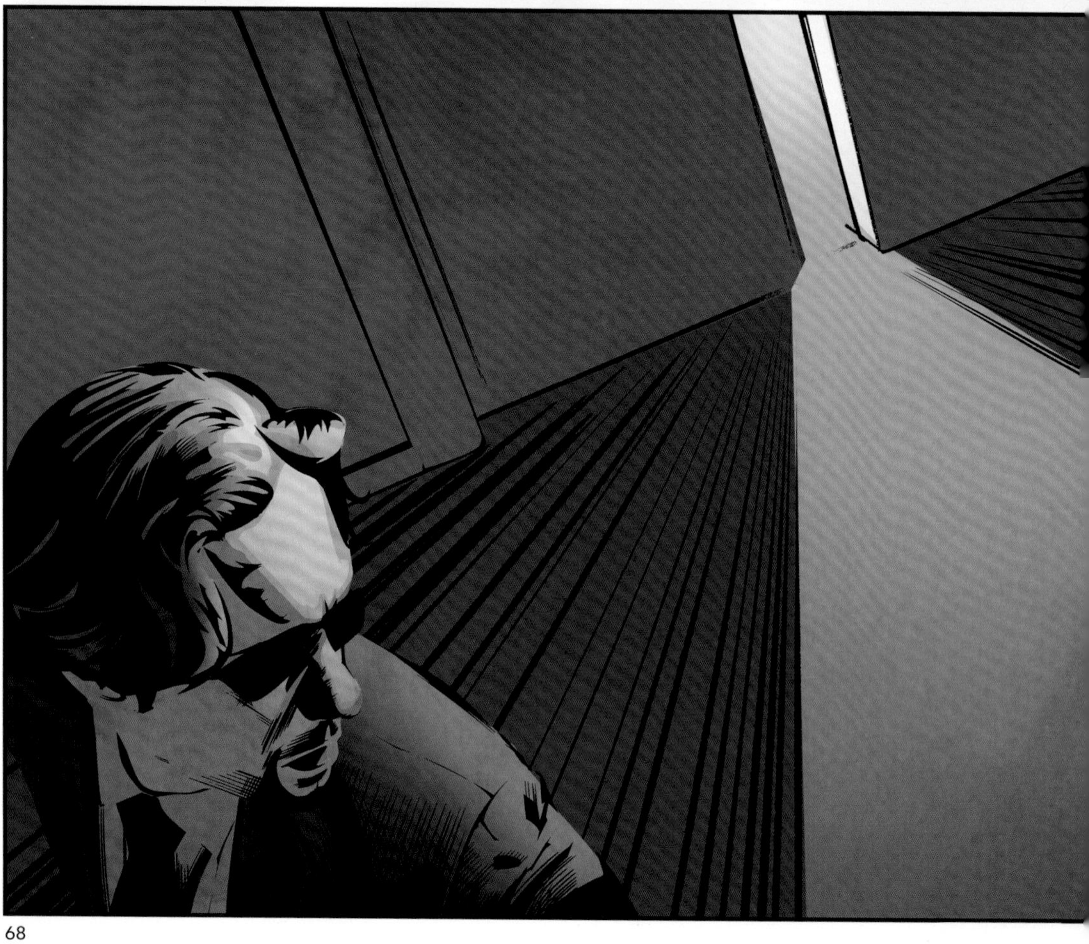

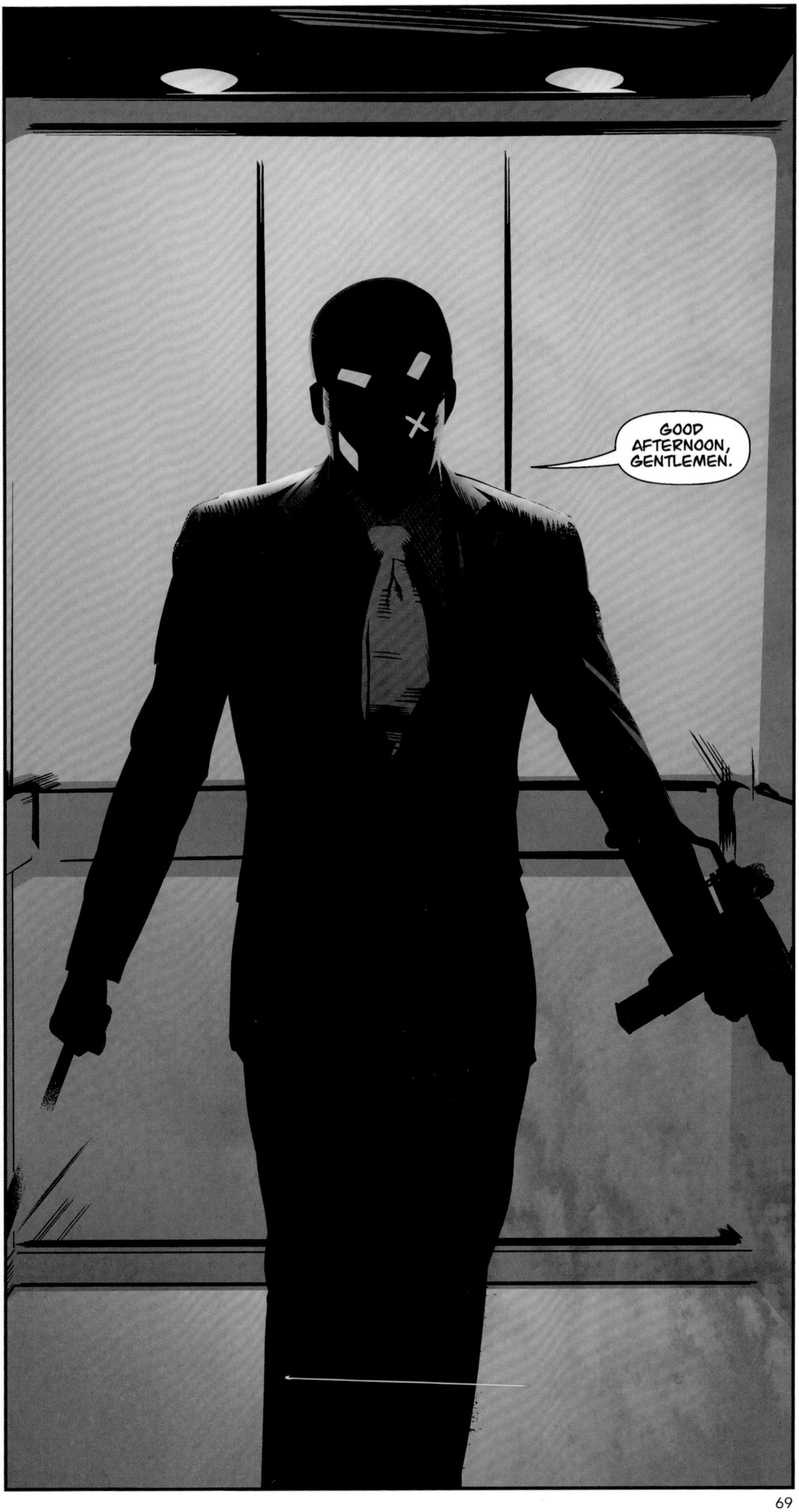
GOOD AFTERNOON, GENTLEMEN.

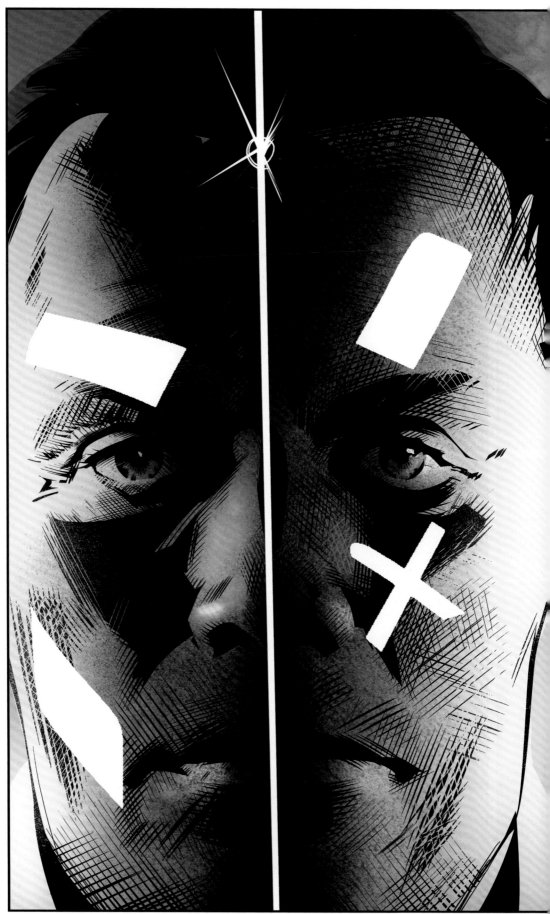

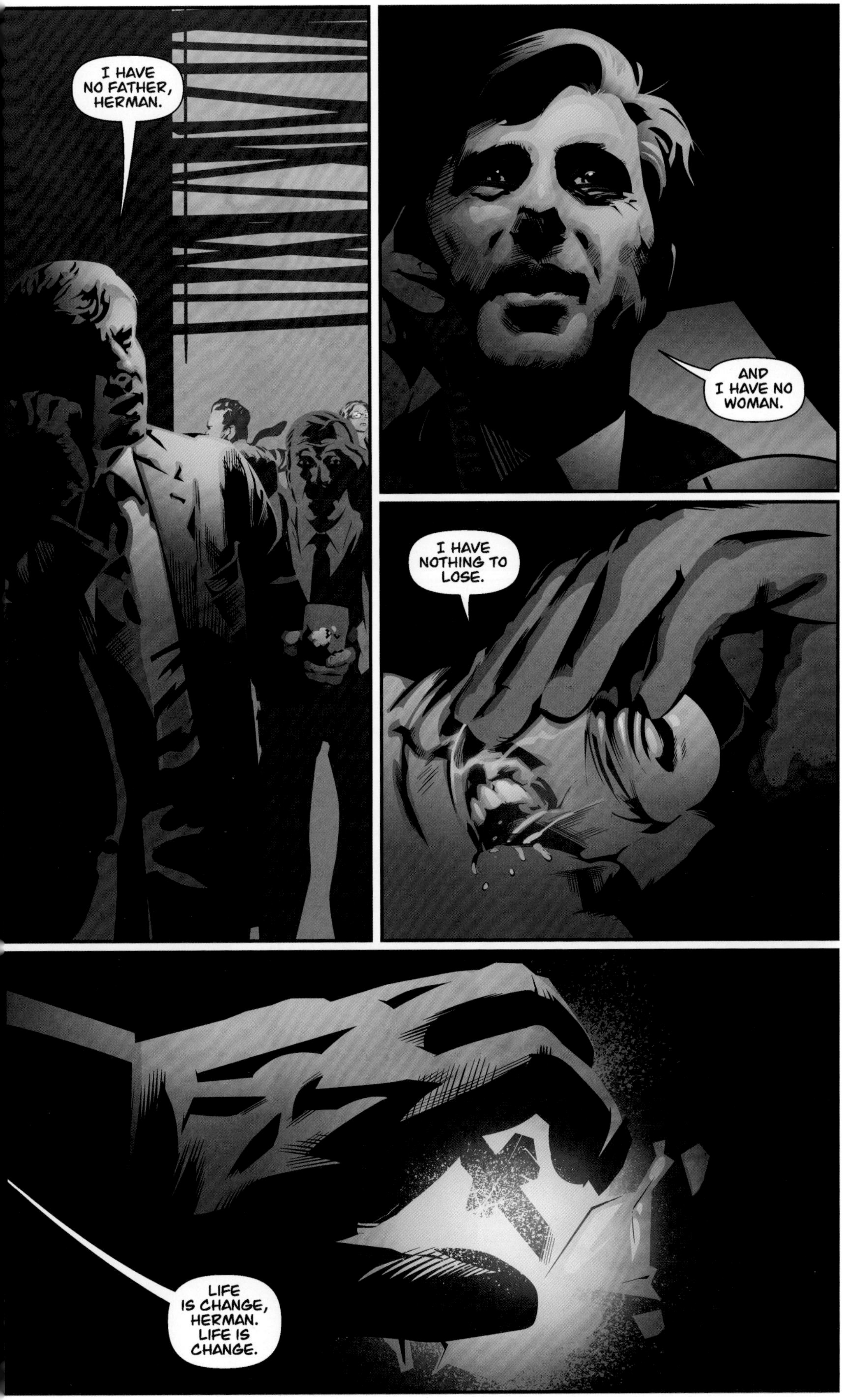
I HAVE NO FATHER, HERMAN.
AND I HAVE NO WOMAN.
I HAVE NOTHING TO LOSE.
LIFE IS CHANGE, HERMAN. LIFE IS CHANGE.

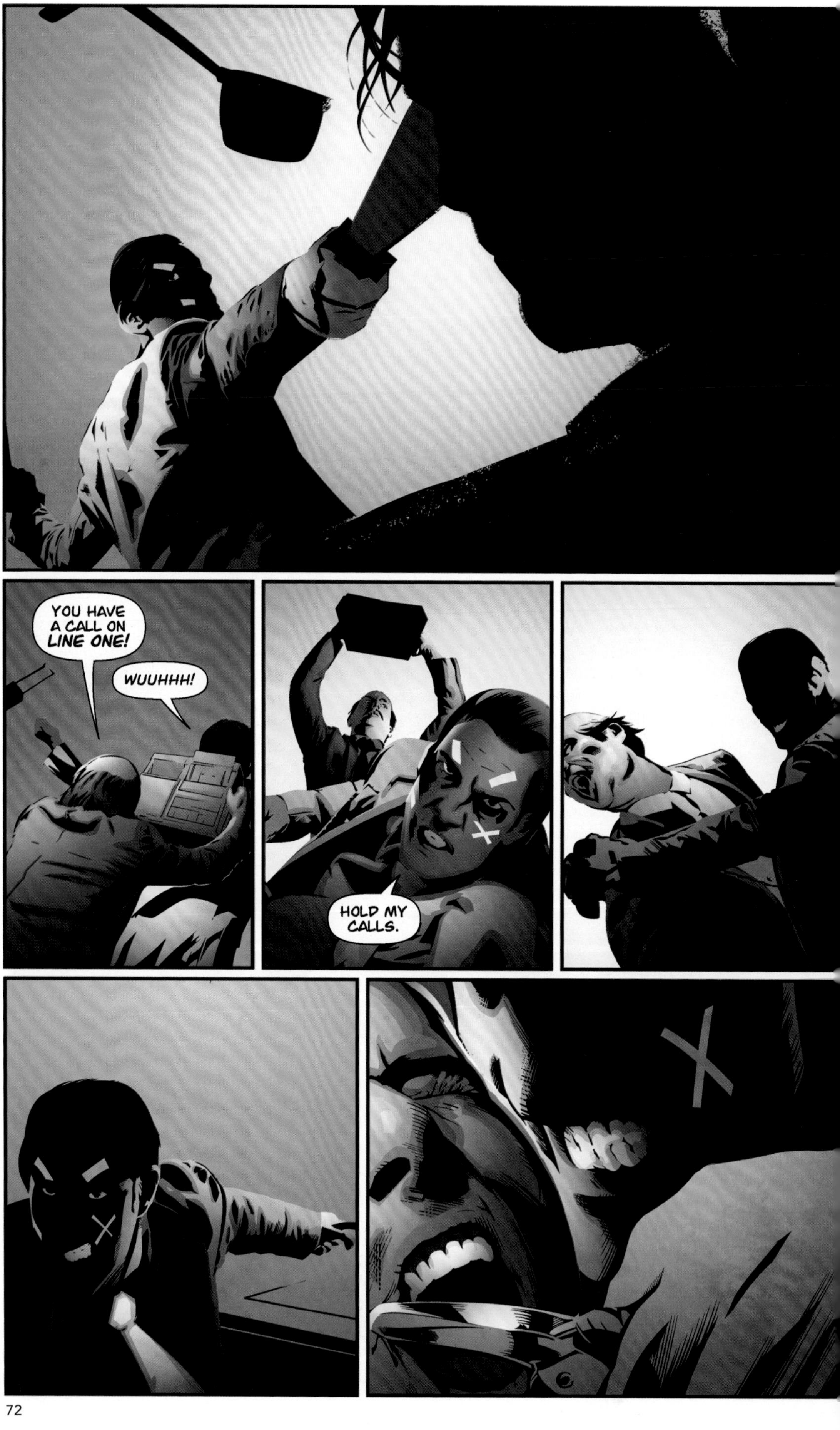
YOU HAVE A CALL ON LINE ONE!
WUUHHH!
HOLD MY CALLS.

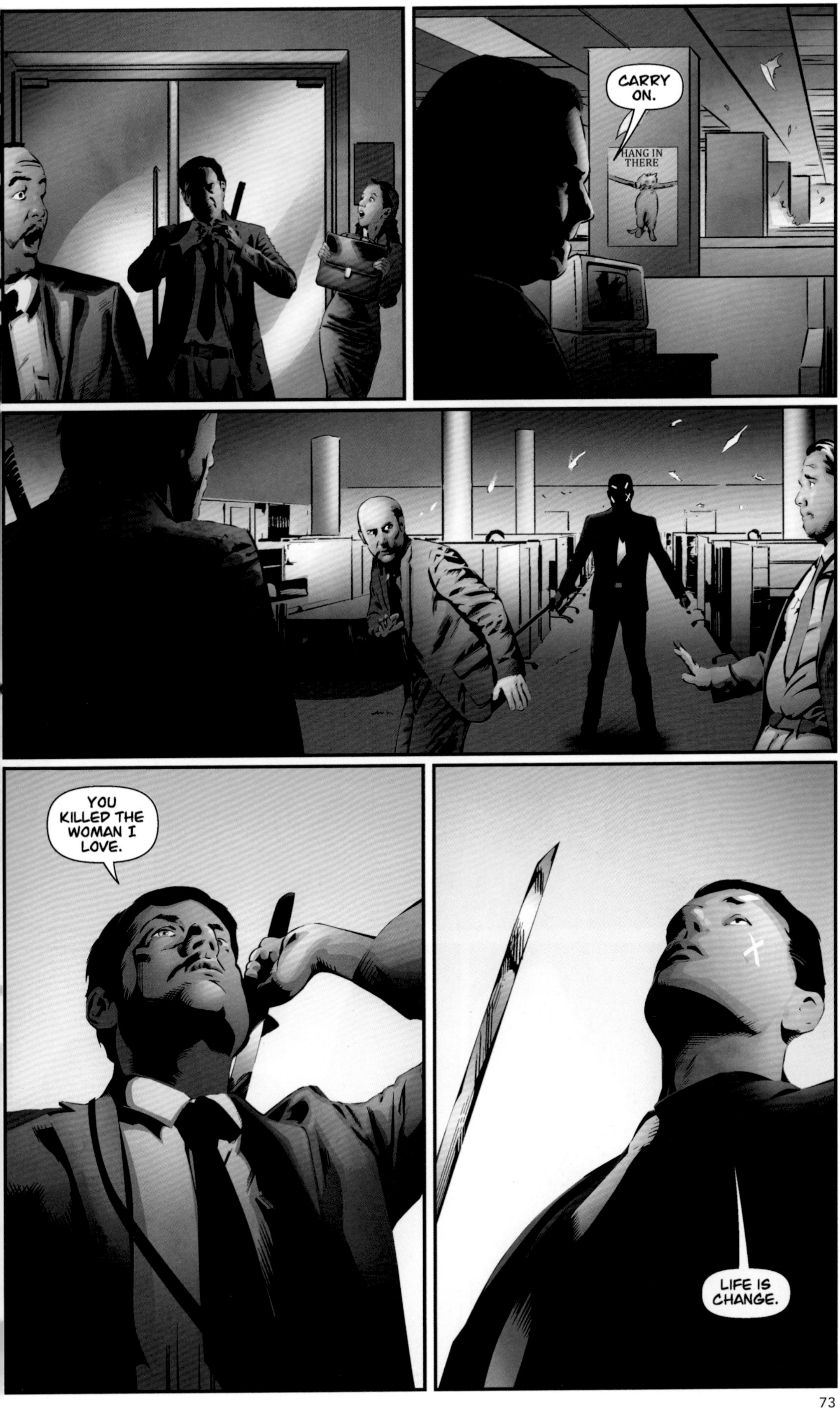
CARRY ON.
HANG IN THERE
YOU KILLED THE WOMAN I LOVE.
LIFE IS CHANGE.

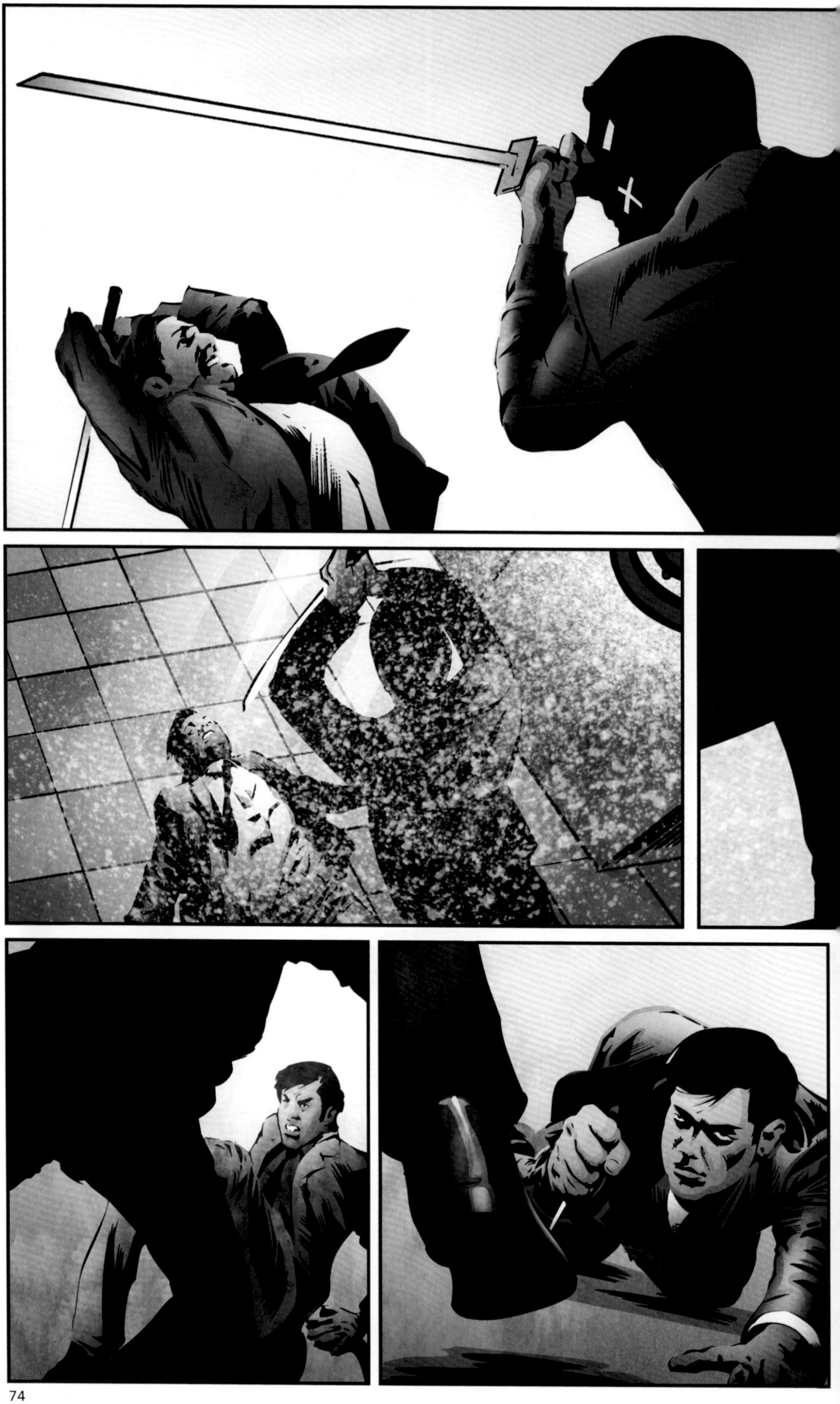

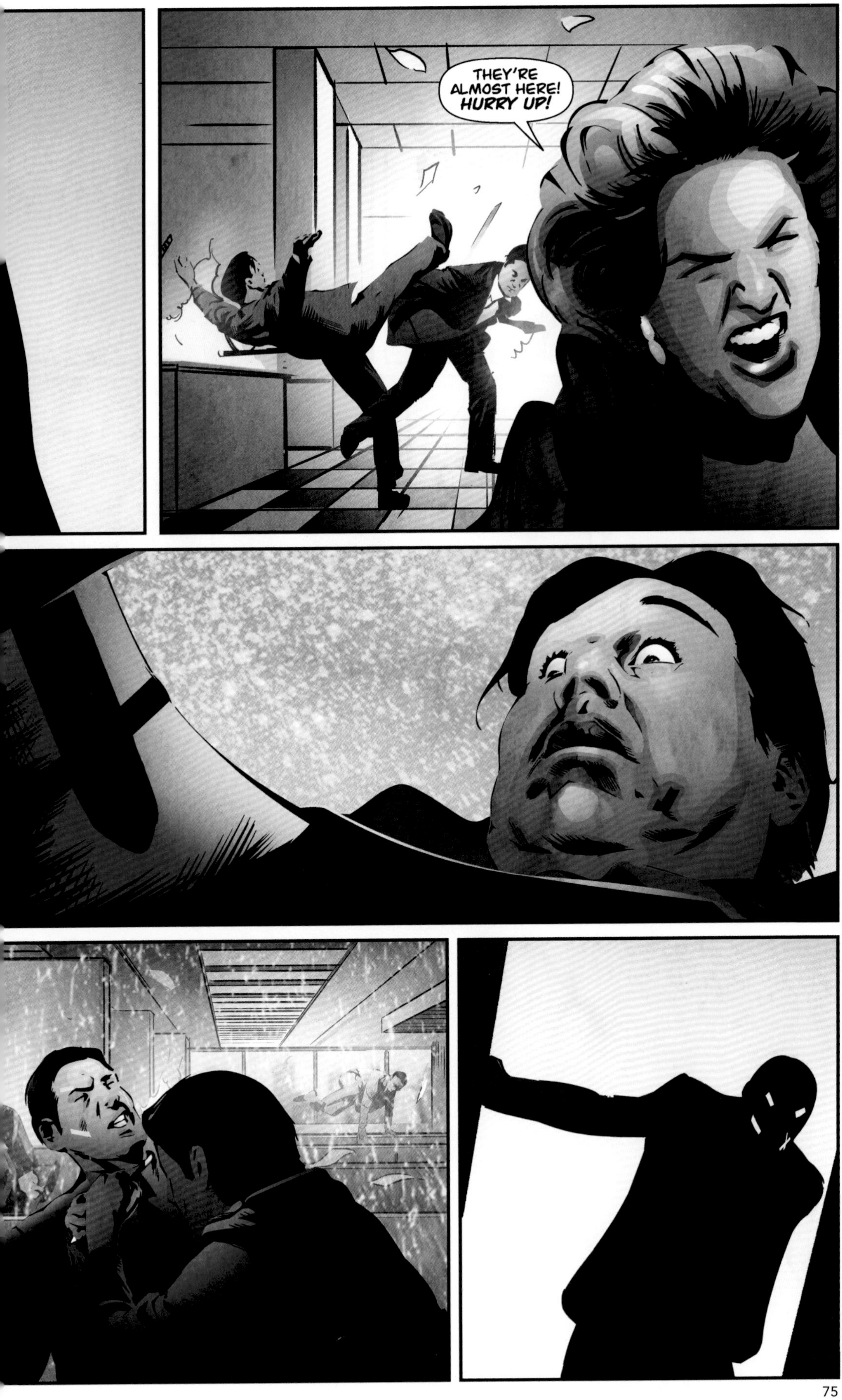
THEY'RE ALMOST HERE! HURRY UP!

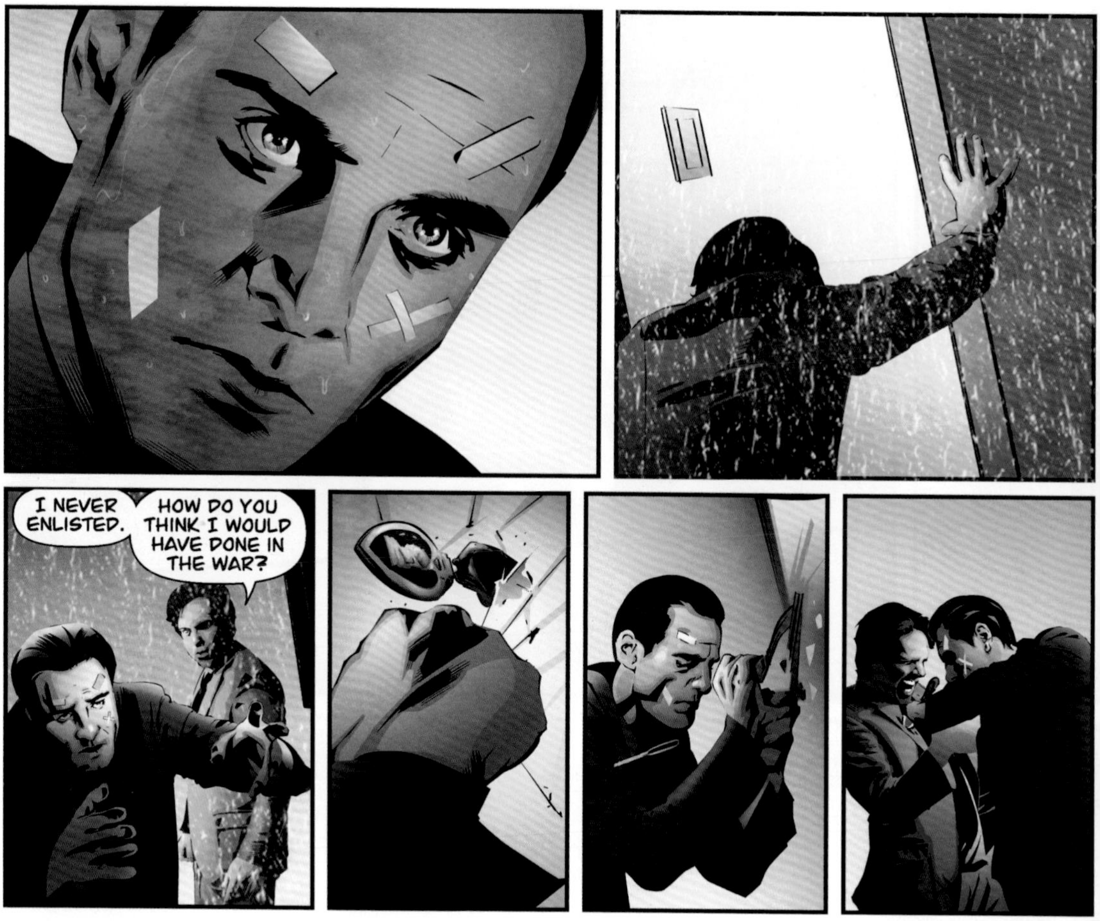
I NEVER ENLISTED.
HOW DO YOU THINK I WOULD HAVE DONE IN THE WAR?

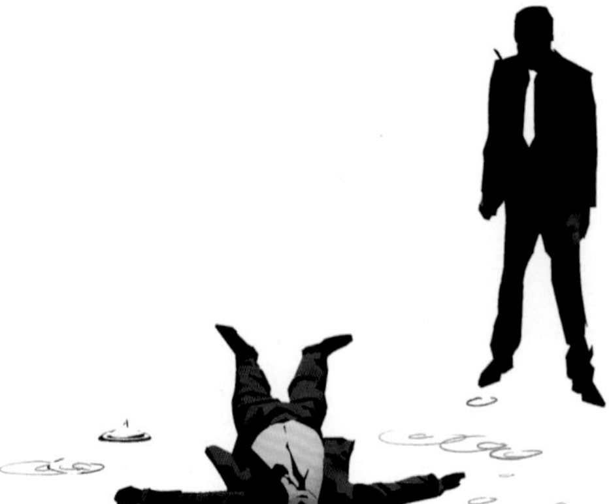

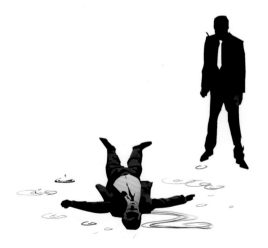

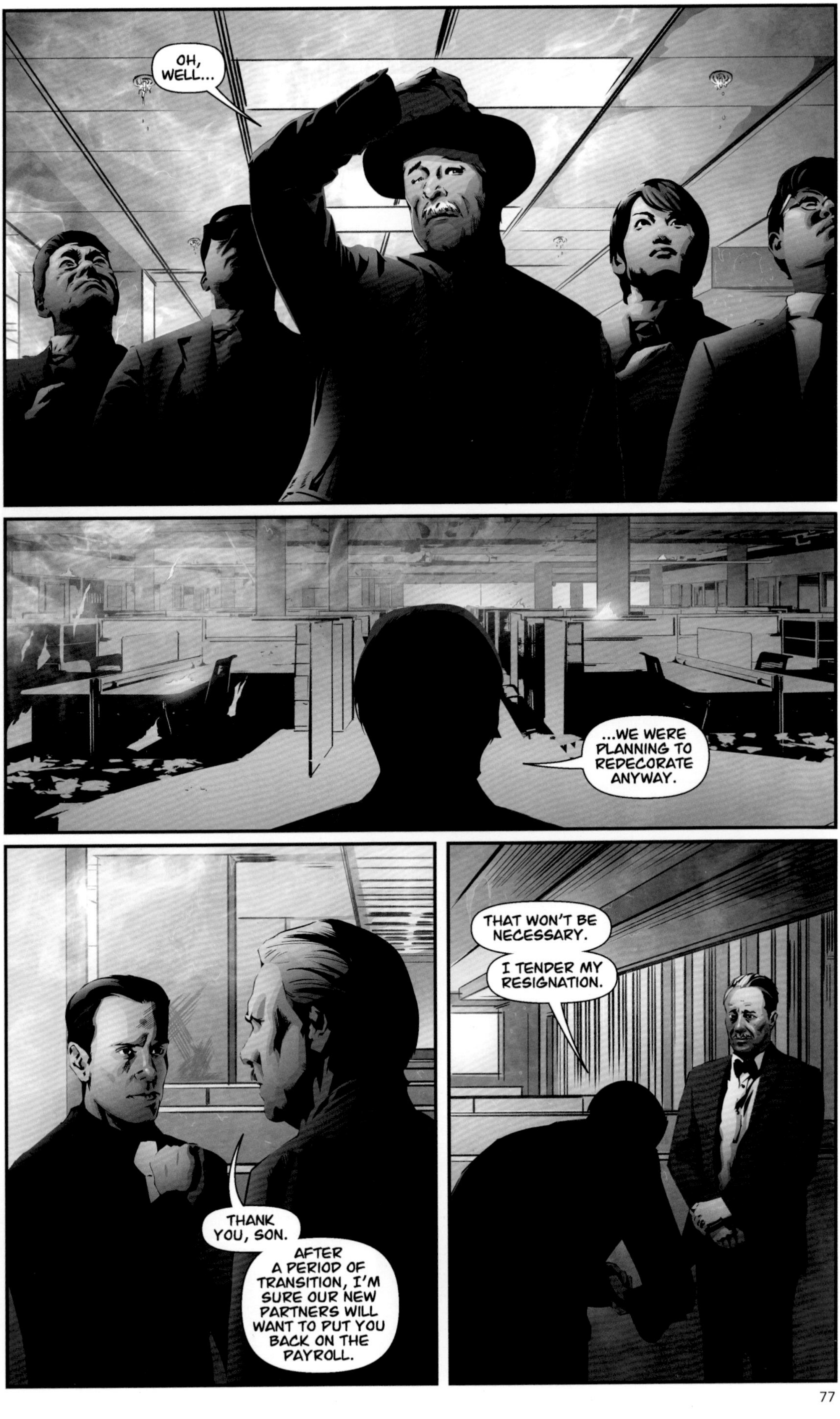
OH, WELL...
...WE WERE PLANNING TO REDECORATE ANYWAY.
THANK YOU, SON.
AFTER A PERIOD OF TRANSITION, I'M SURE OUR NEW PARTNERS WILL WANT TO PUT YOU BACK ON THE PAYROLL.
THAT WON'T BE NECESSARY.
I TENDER MY RESIGNATION.

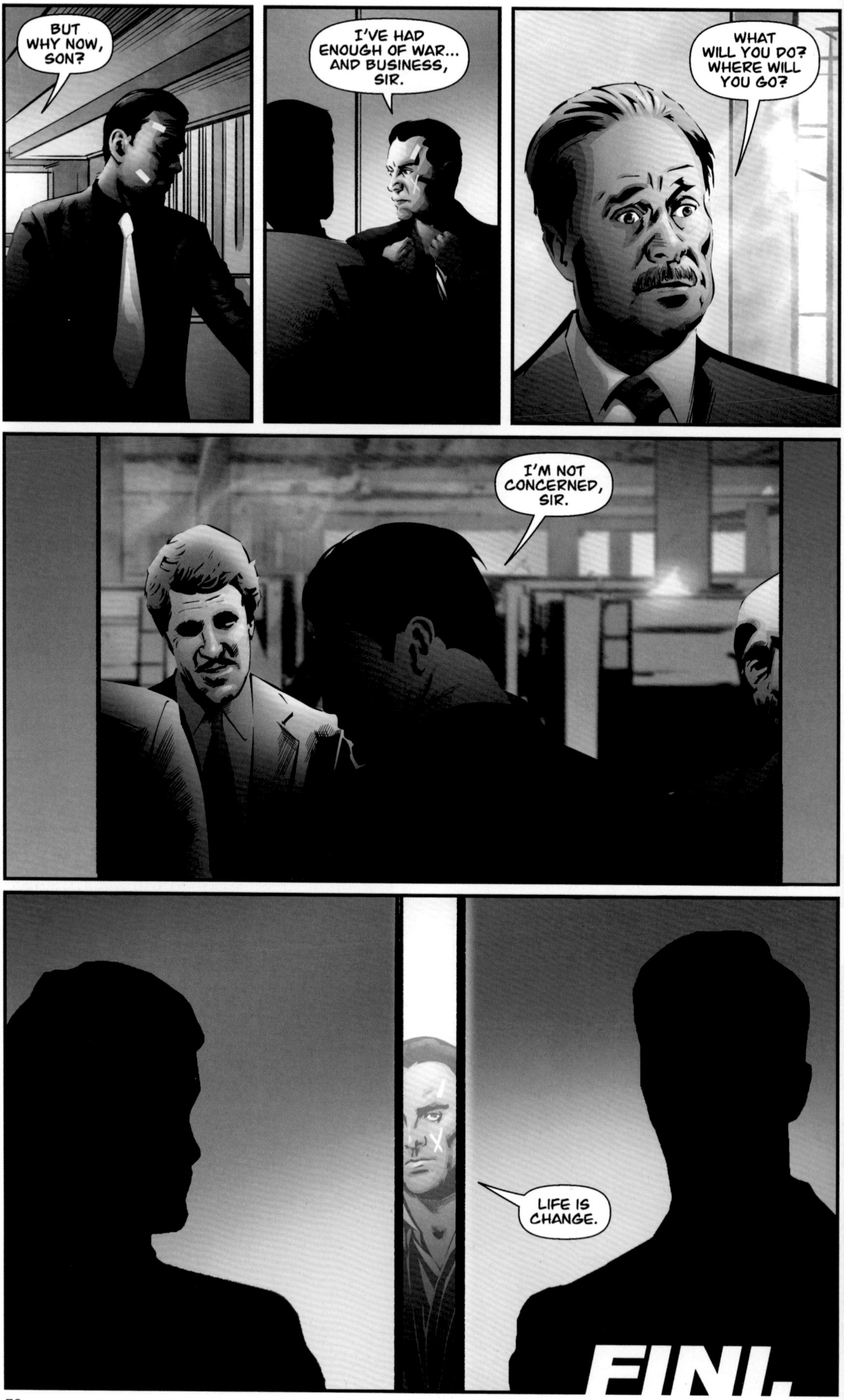
BUT WHY NOW, SON?
I'VE HAD ENOUGH OF WAR... AND BUSINESS, SIR.
WHAT WILL YOU DO? WHERE WILL YOU GO?
I'M NOT CONCERNED, SIR.
LIFE IS CHANGE.
FINI.

# THE SUIT™

## SKETCHBOOK

## LAYOUTS by Dennis Calero

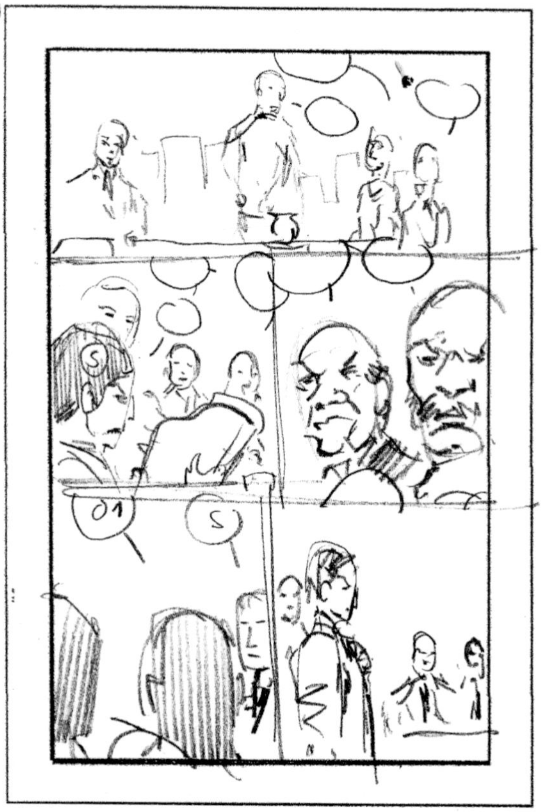

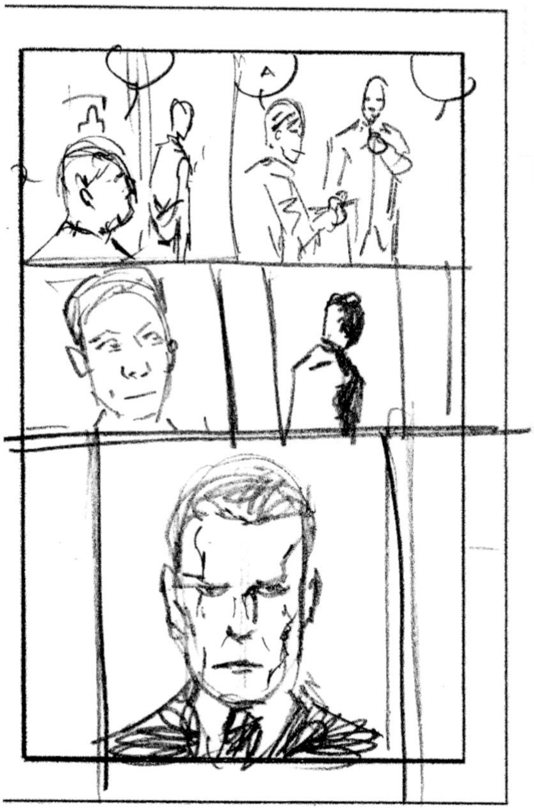

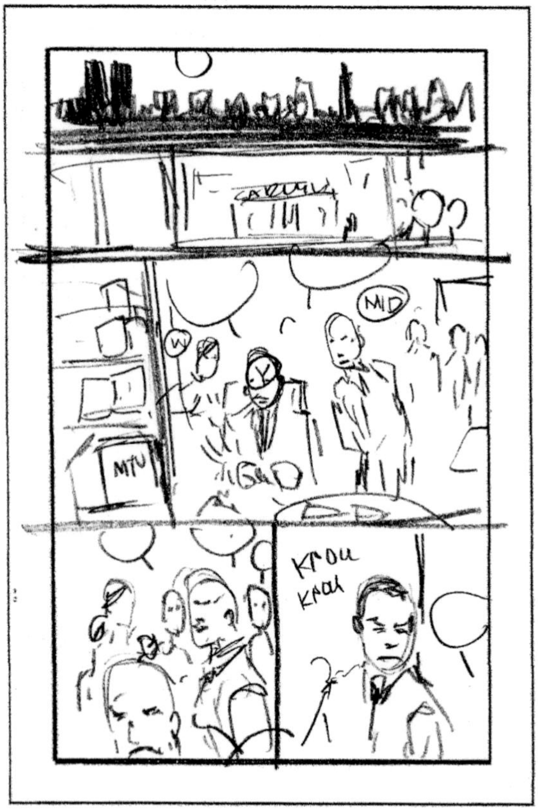

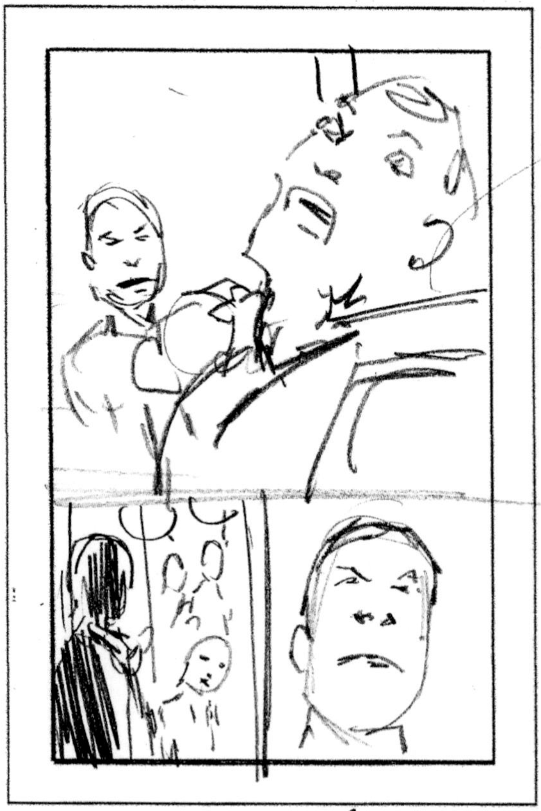

Layouts, for me, are the hard part. Even before doing them, the decision as to how to approach storytelling is akin to how you shoot a film, but even more so.

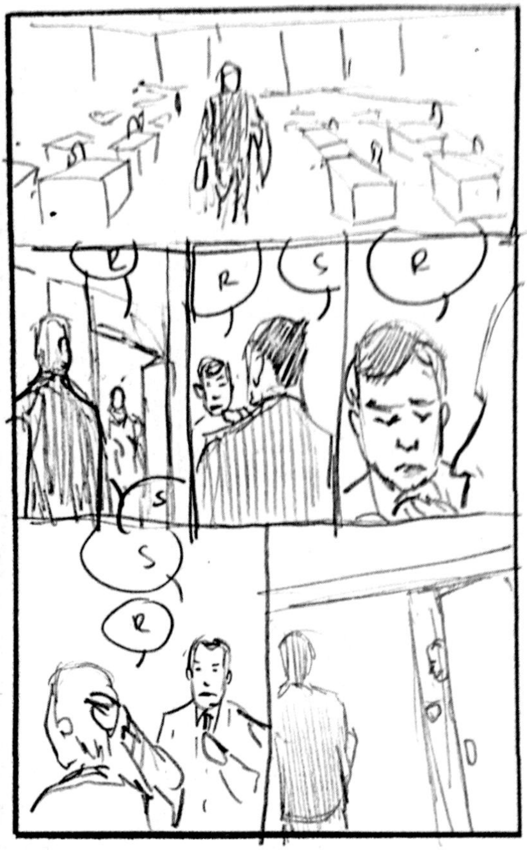

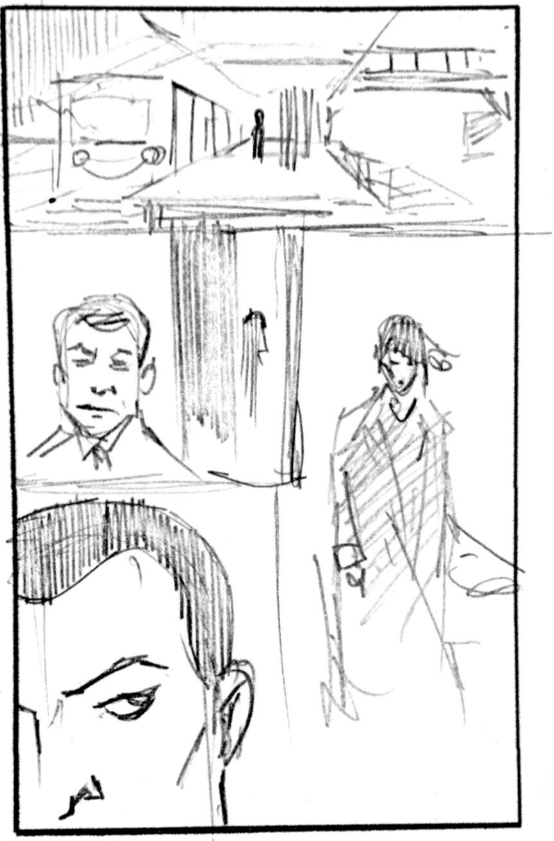

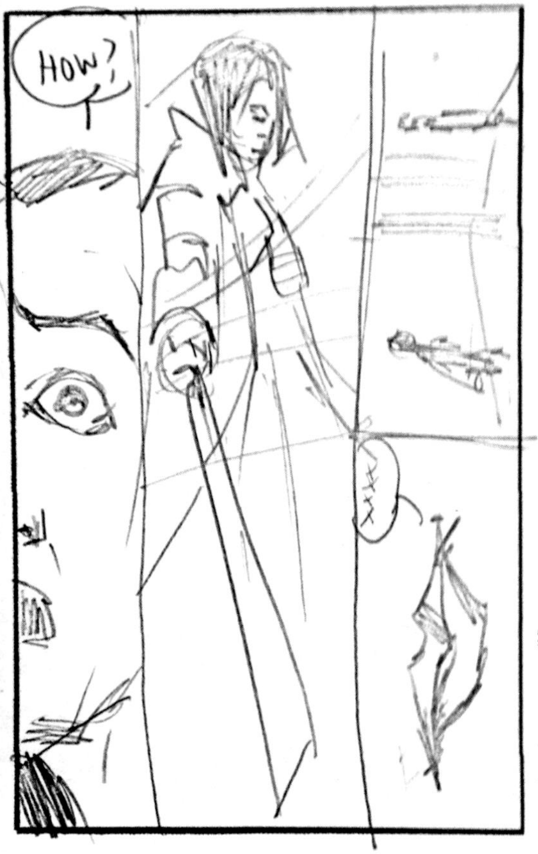
HOW?

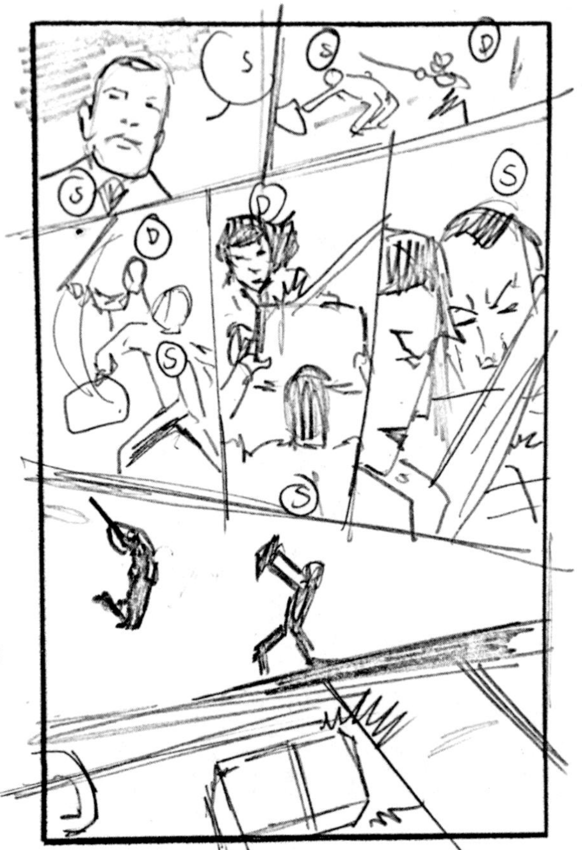

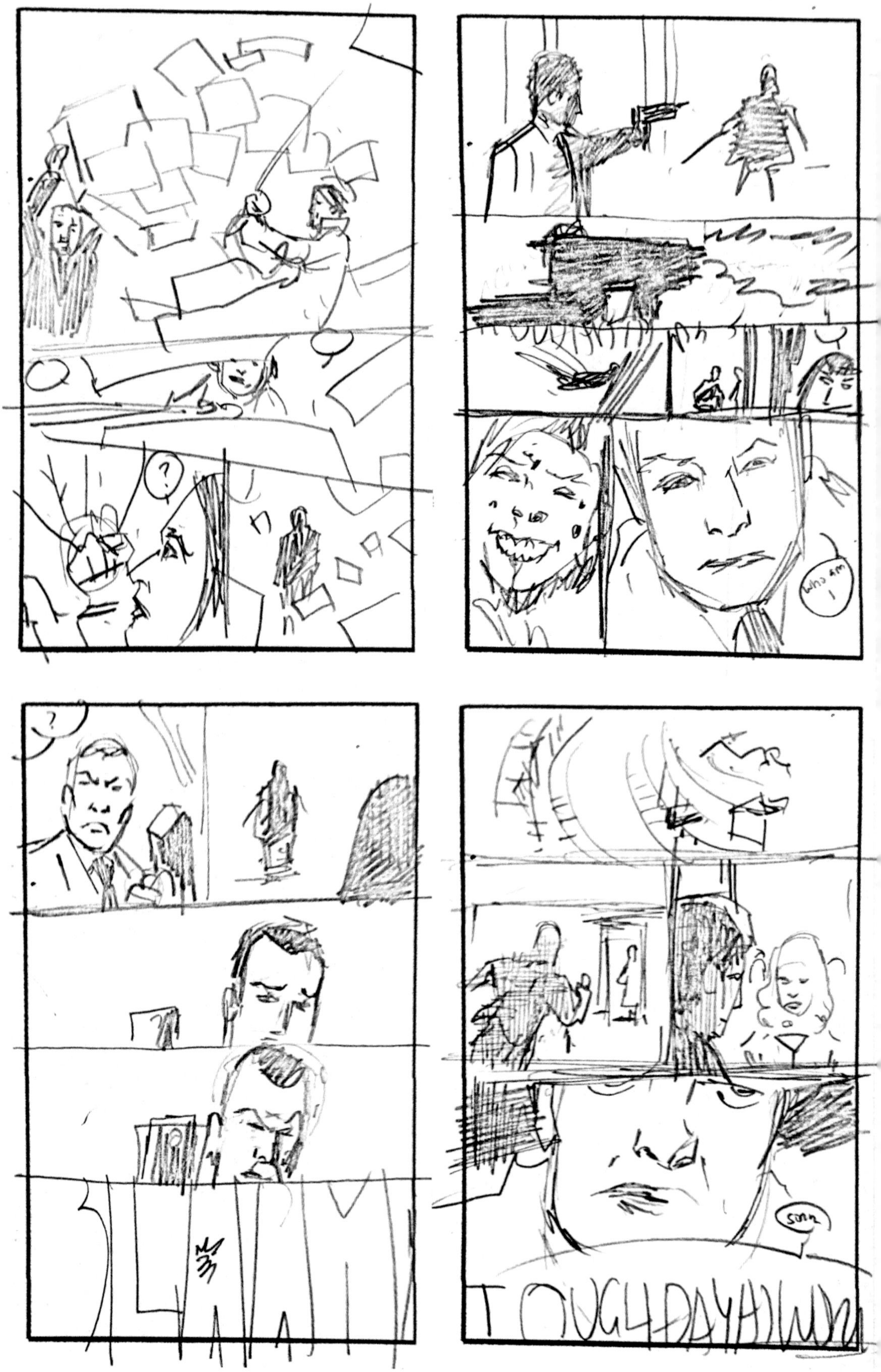
?
?
Who am I


In a film, you essentially have one panel shape. But in comics, you can break up the standard page any number of ways, deeply affecting the reader's experience.

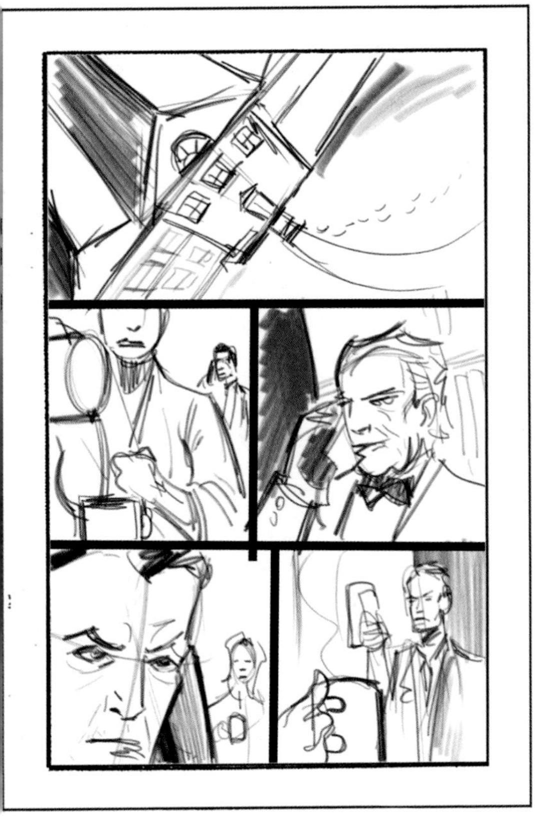

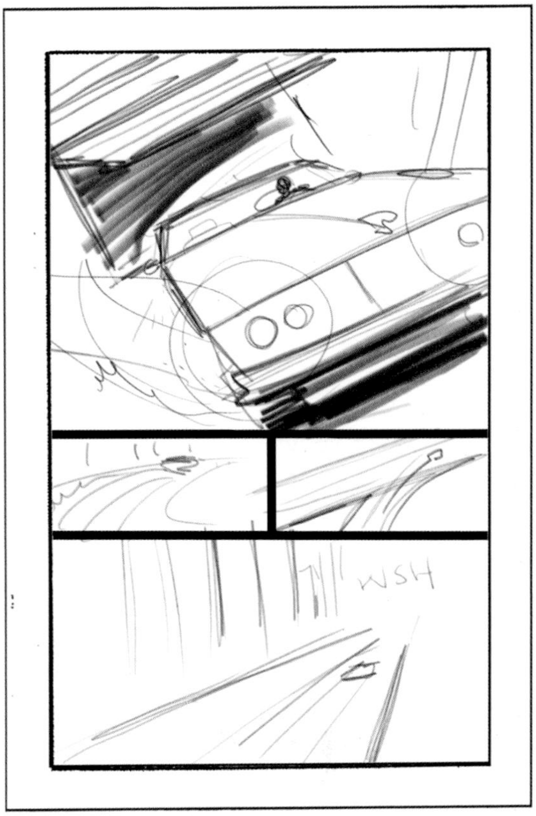
WSH

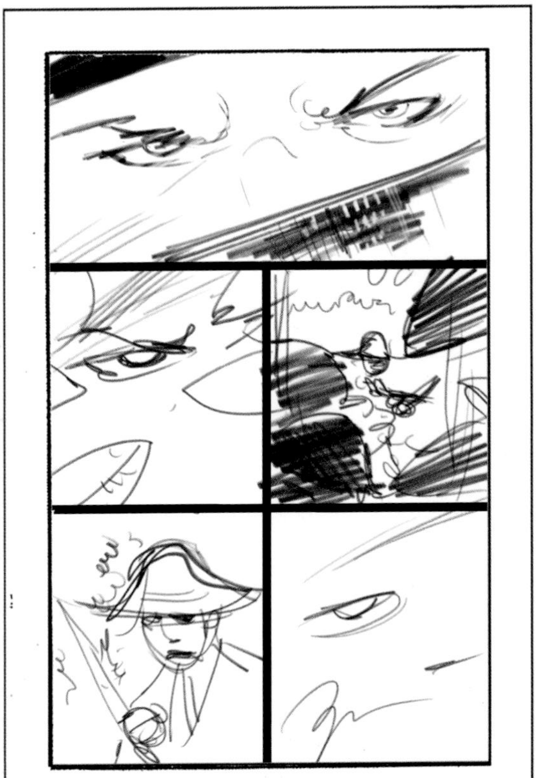

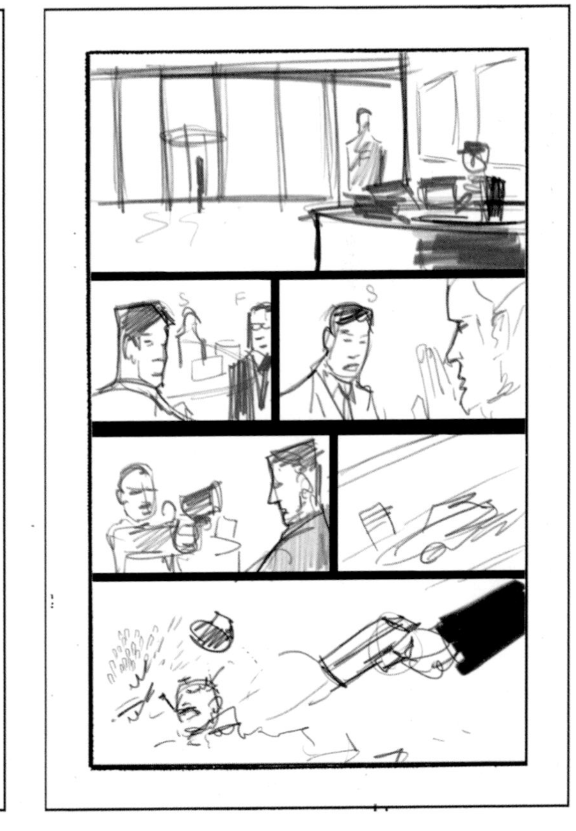

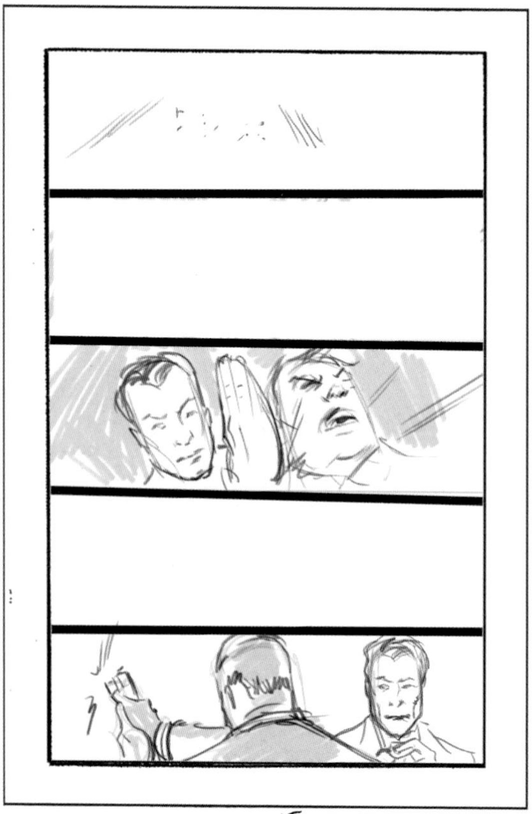

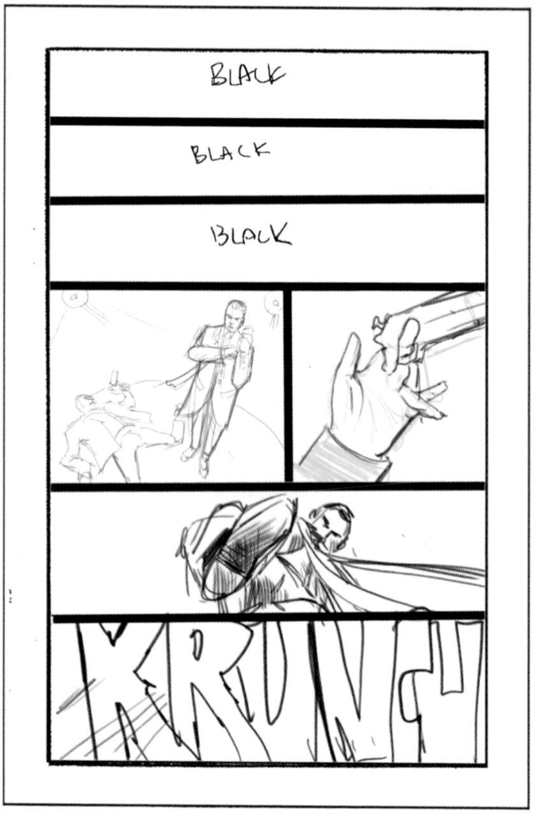
BLACK
BLACK
BLACK
KRUNCH

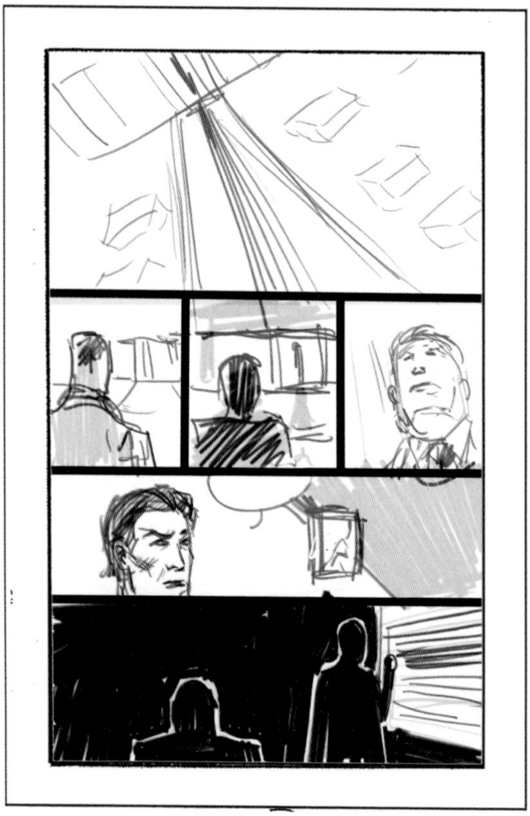

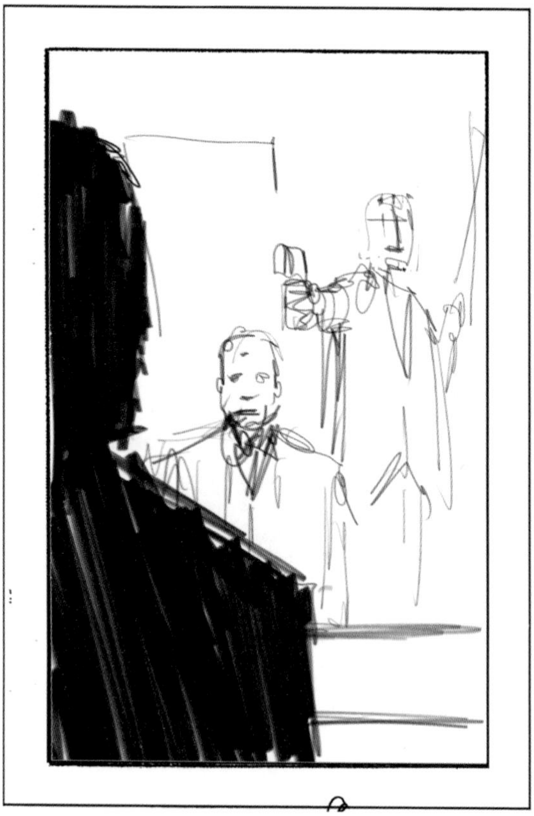

I decided to play The Suit "straight" in order to, hopefully, lend an air of dream-like strangeness. Present a world that feels as real as possible, but where these odd things happen.

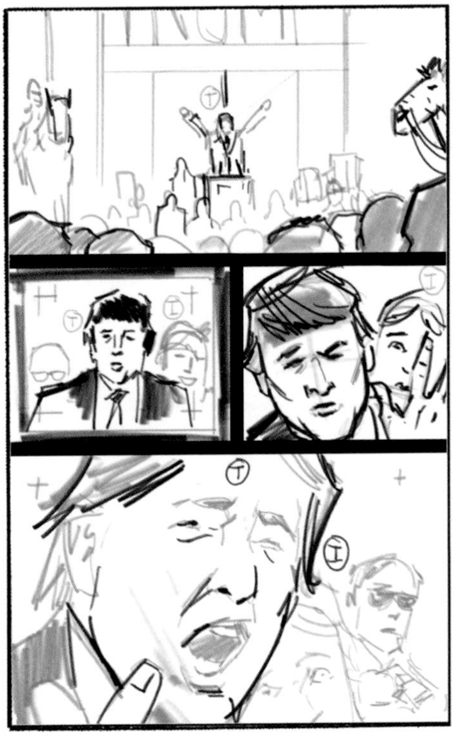

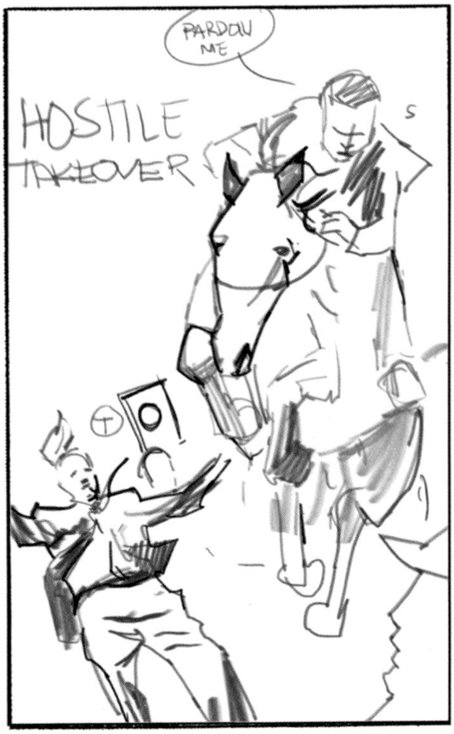
PARDON ME
HOSTILE TAKEOVER

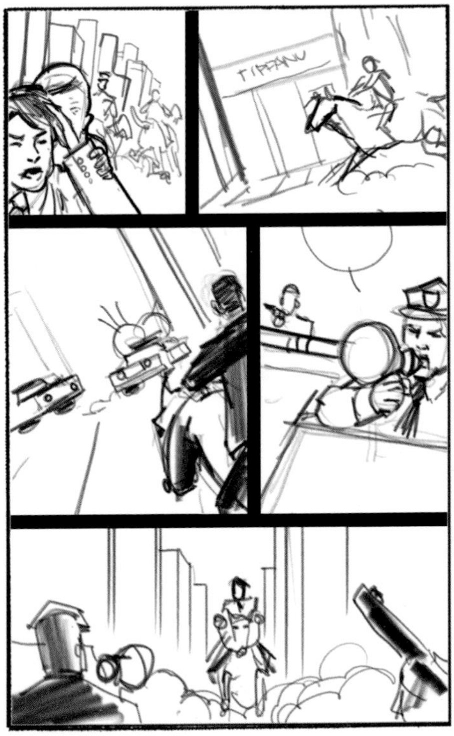

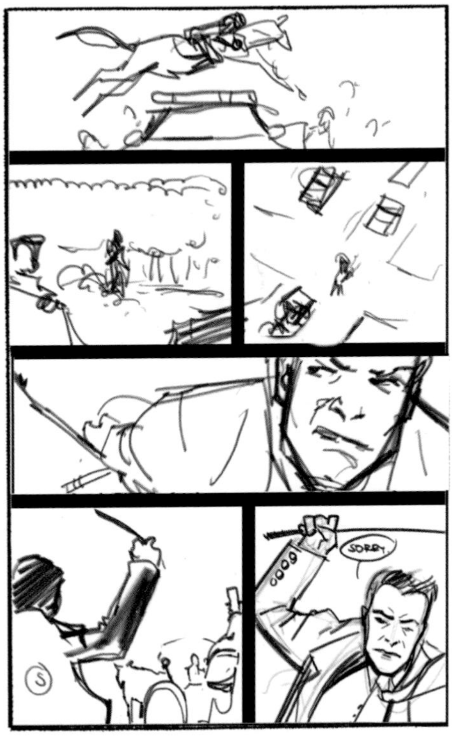
SORRY

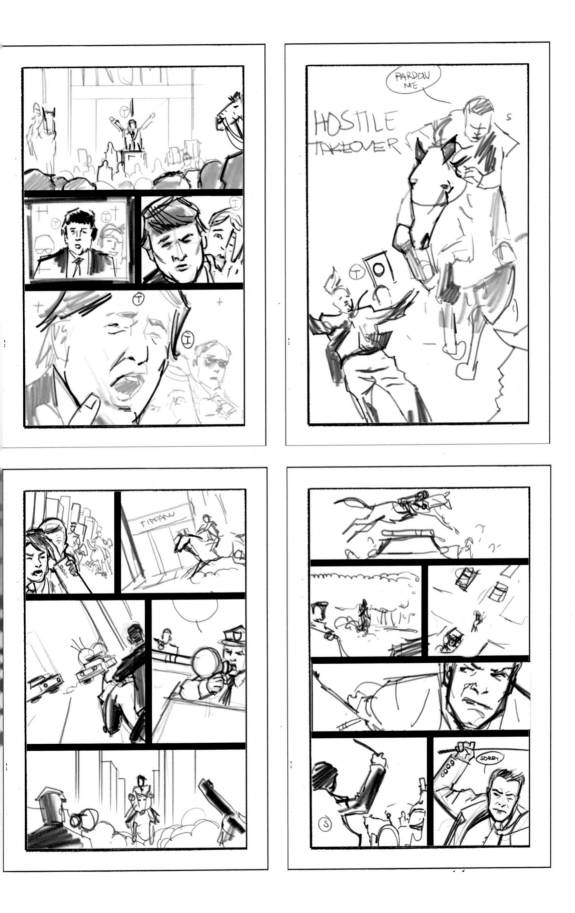

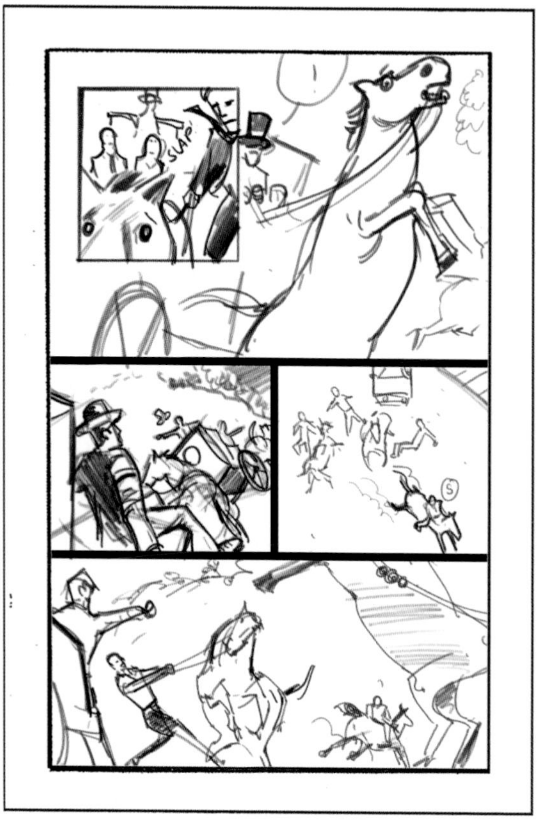
!
SLAP

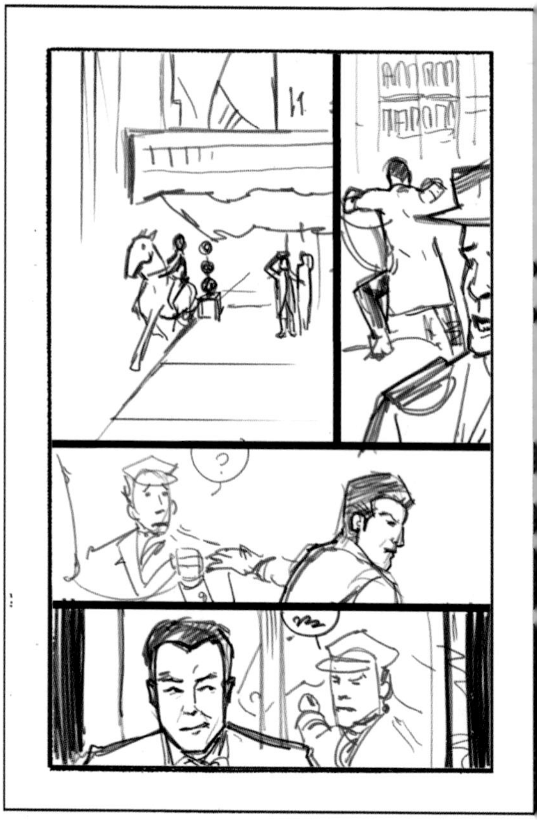
?

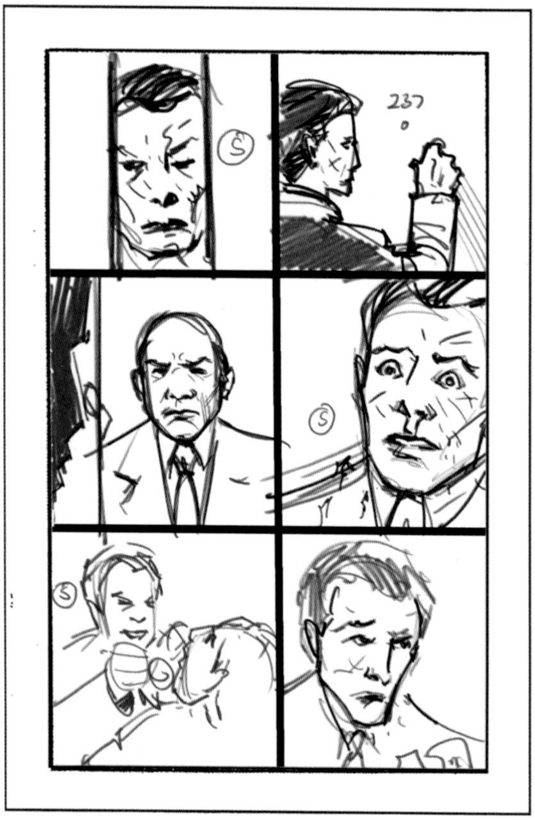
237

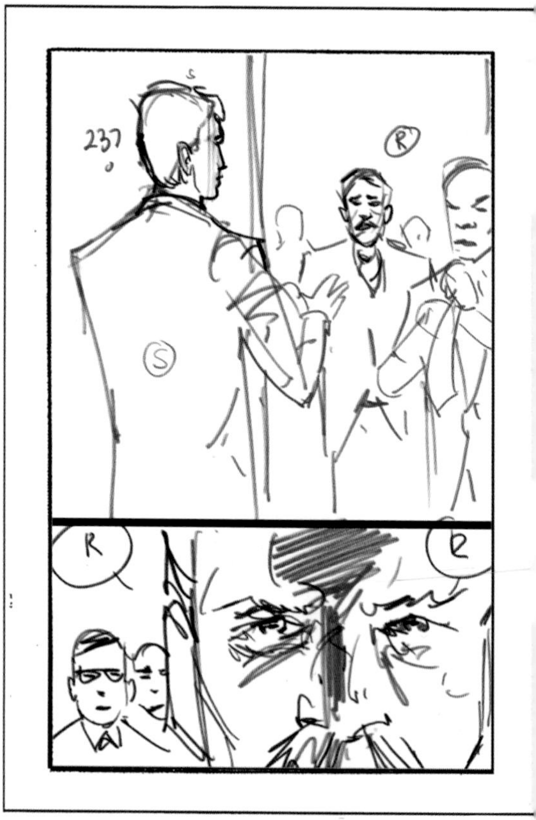
237

My layouts are always fairly loose, and generally I don't listen to any music with lyrics, or podcasts, or anything with ideas that are trying to engage my brain while I'm working this stuff out. After this stage, it's labor.

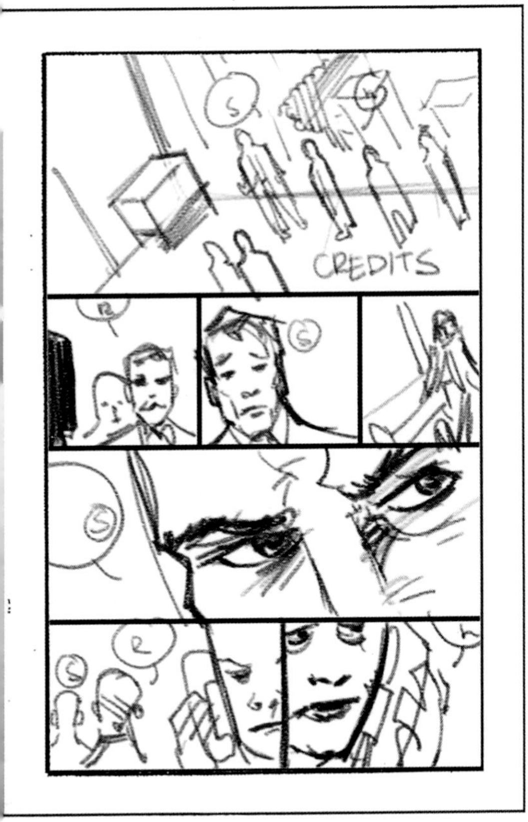
CREDITS

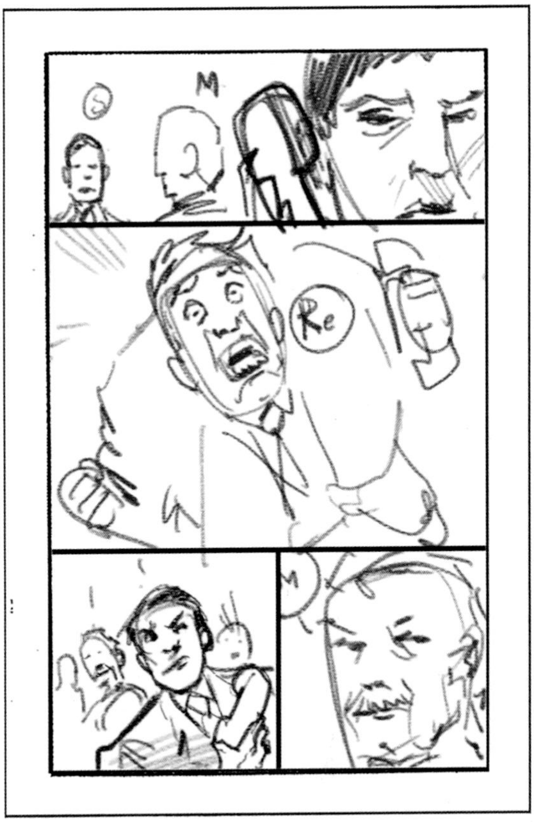

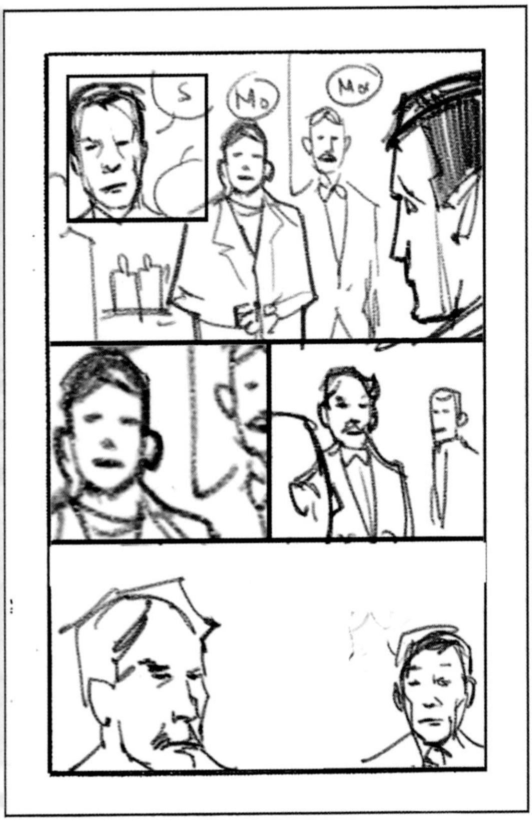

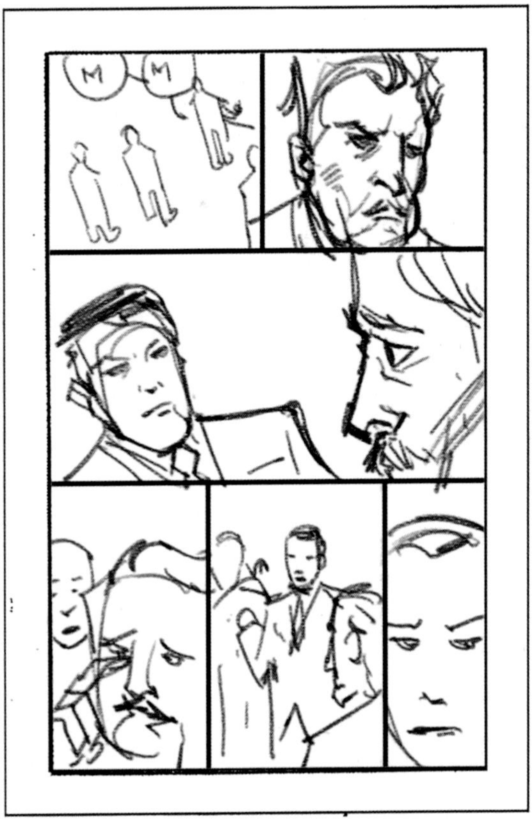

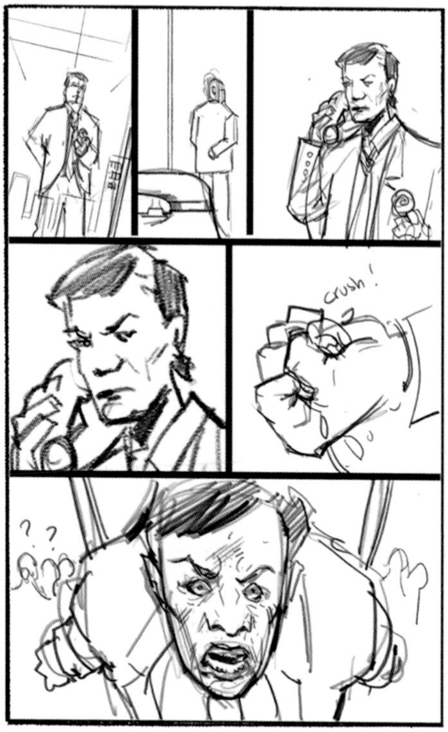
crush!
? ?

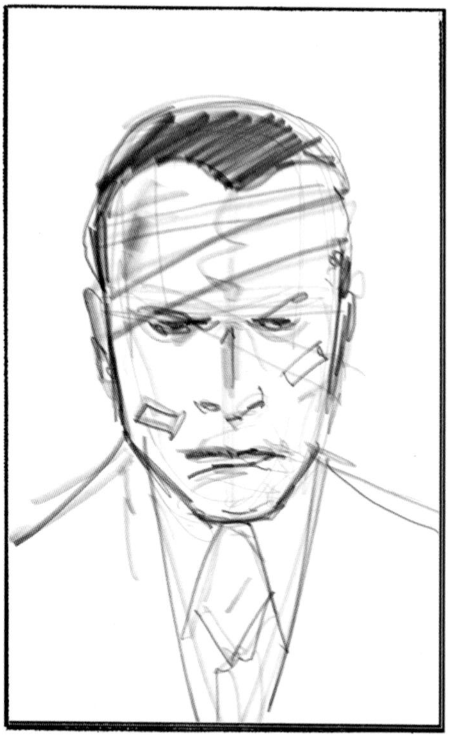

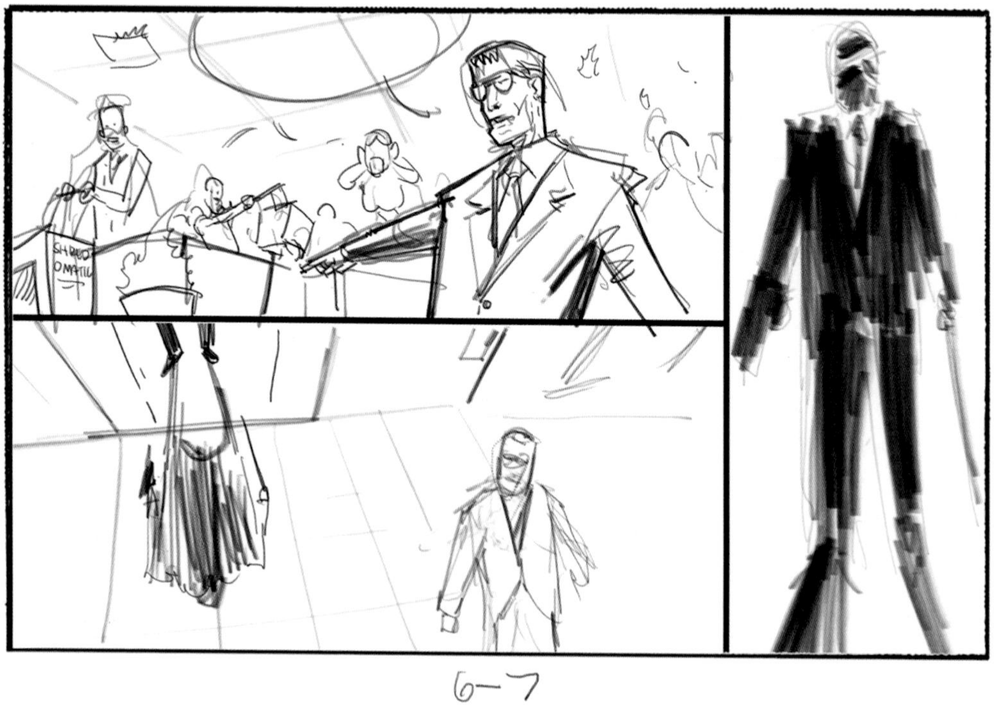

6–7

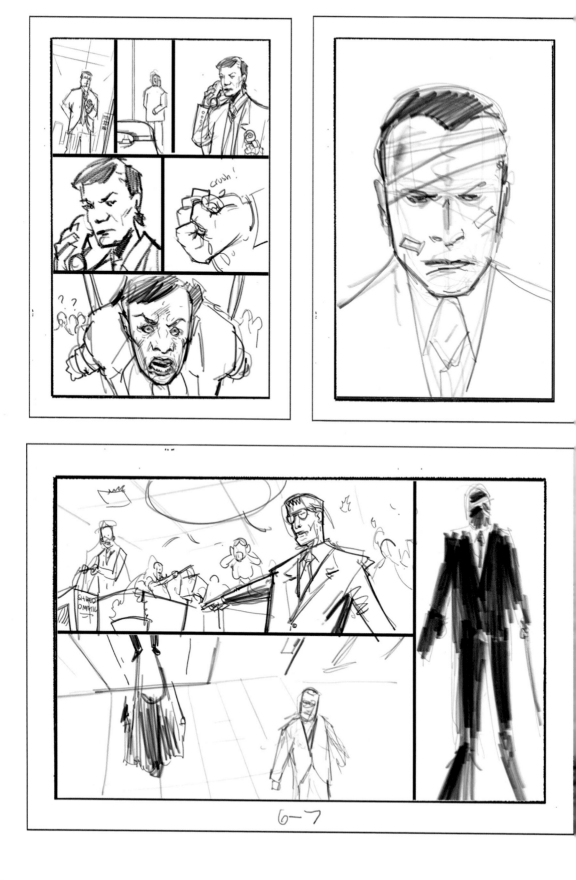

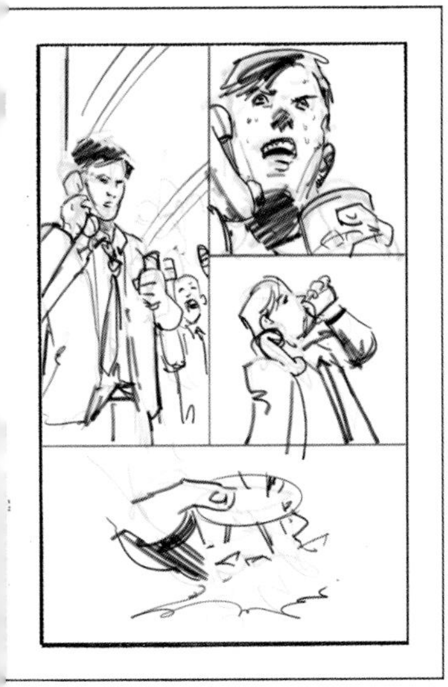

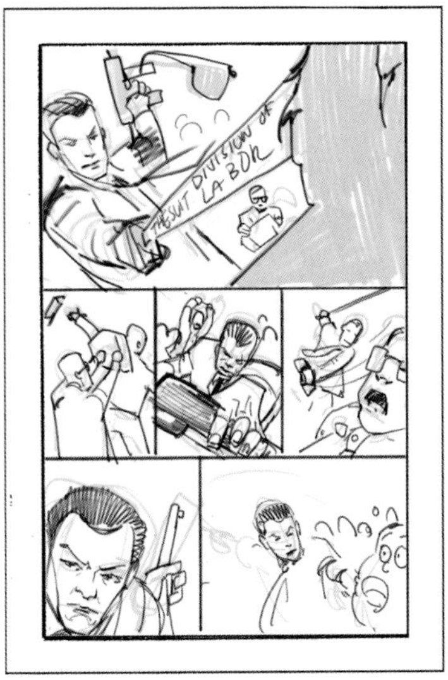
THE SUIT DIVISION OF
LA BOR

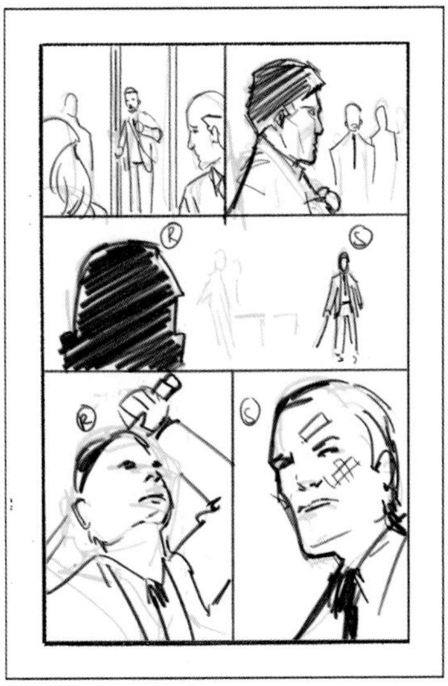
R
S
R
S

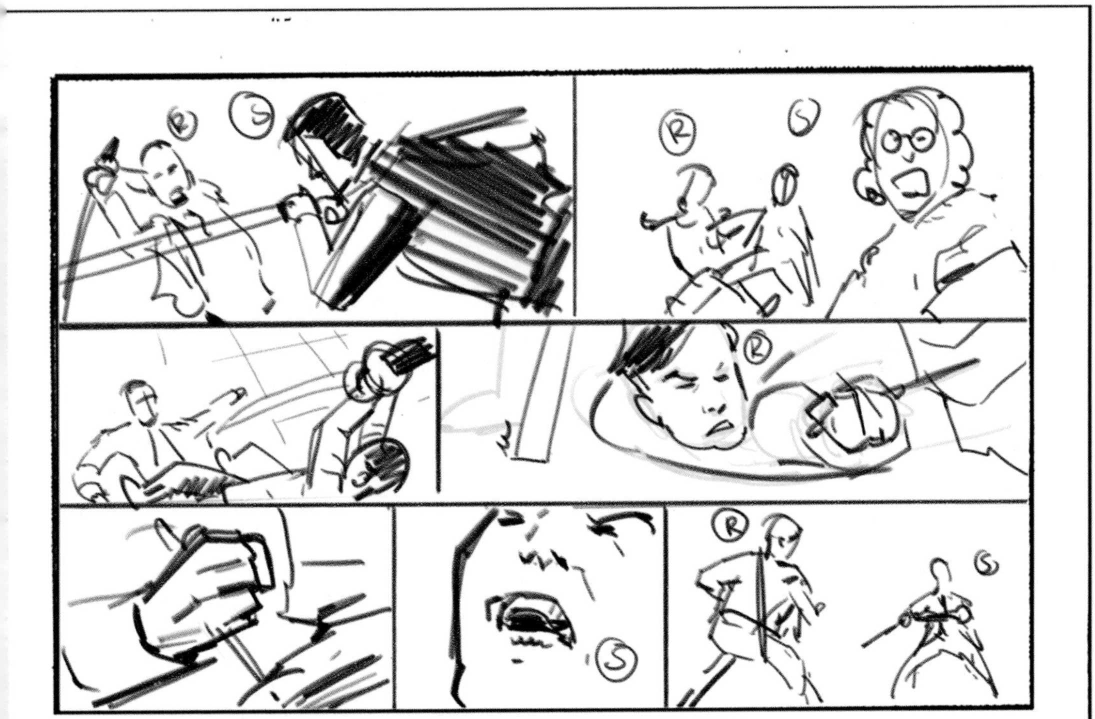
R
S
R
S
R
S
R
S

# COVER SKETCHES
## by Dennis Calero

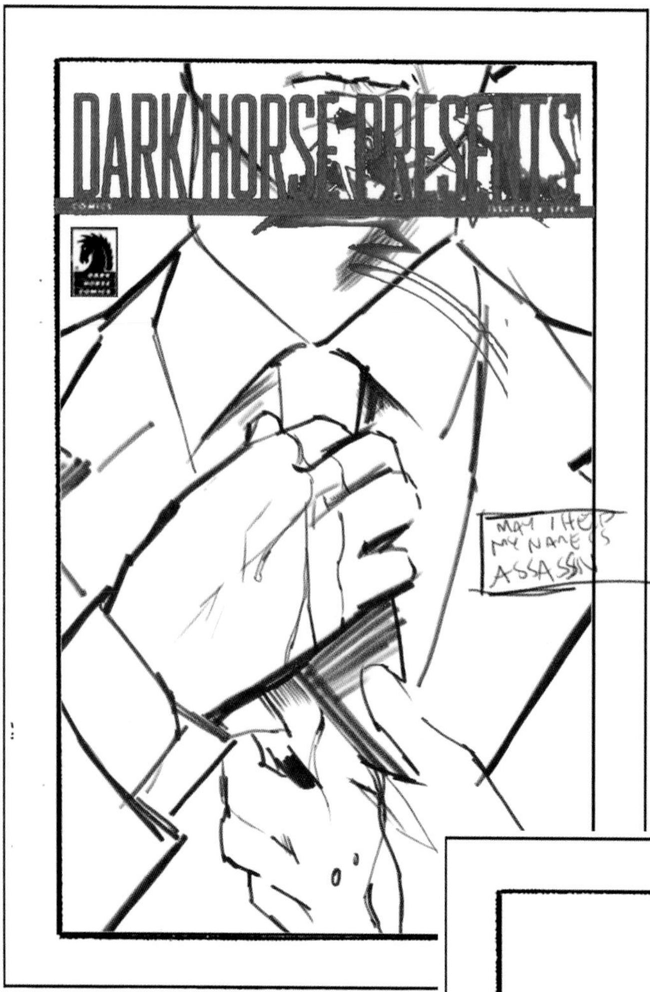
DARK HORSE PRESENTS
MAY I HELP
MY NAME IS
ASSASSIN

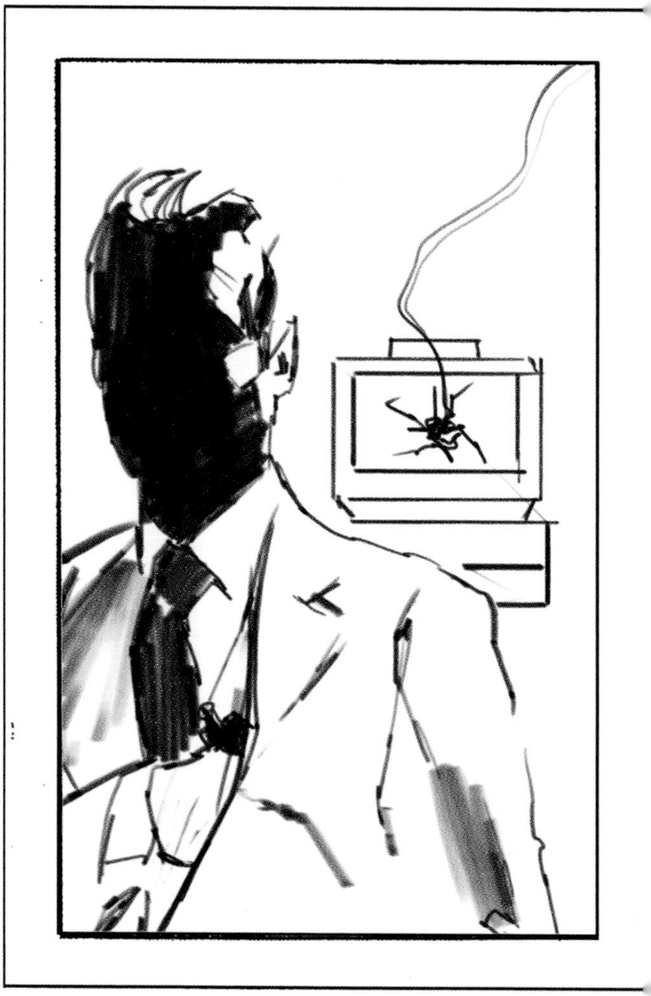

I wanted to do something that evoked possibly the most eighties of the pop artists, Patrick Nagle. His sharp-as-razors lines deftly depicted the machine-like slickness of the yuppie ideal. Using this to illustrate a man of incomparable personal machine-like violence seemed interesting to me.

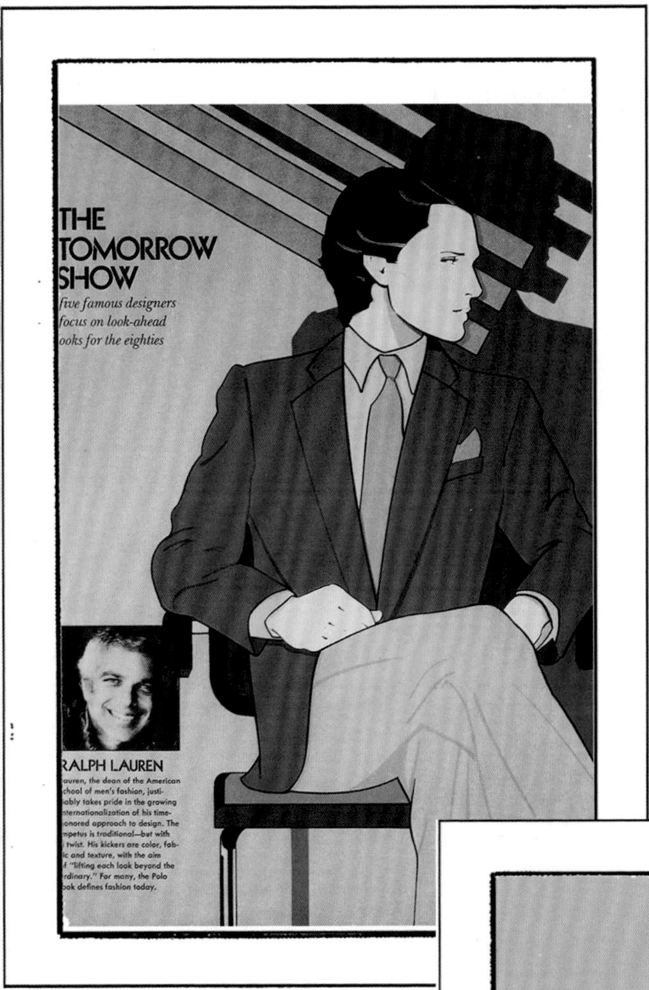

THE
TOMORROW
SHOW

*five famous designers focus on look-ahead ooks for the eighties*

RALPH LAUREN

auren, the dean of the American chool of men's fashion, justiiably takes pride in the growing nternationalization of his timeonored approach to design. The mpetus is traditional—but with twist. His kickers are color, fabic and texture, with the aim f "lifting each look beyond the rdinary." For many, the Polo ook defines fashion today.

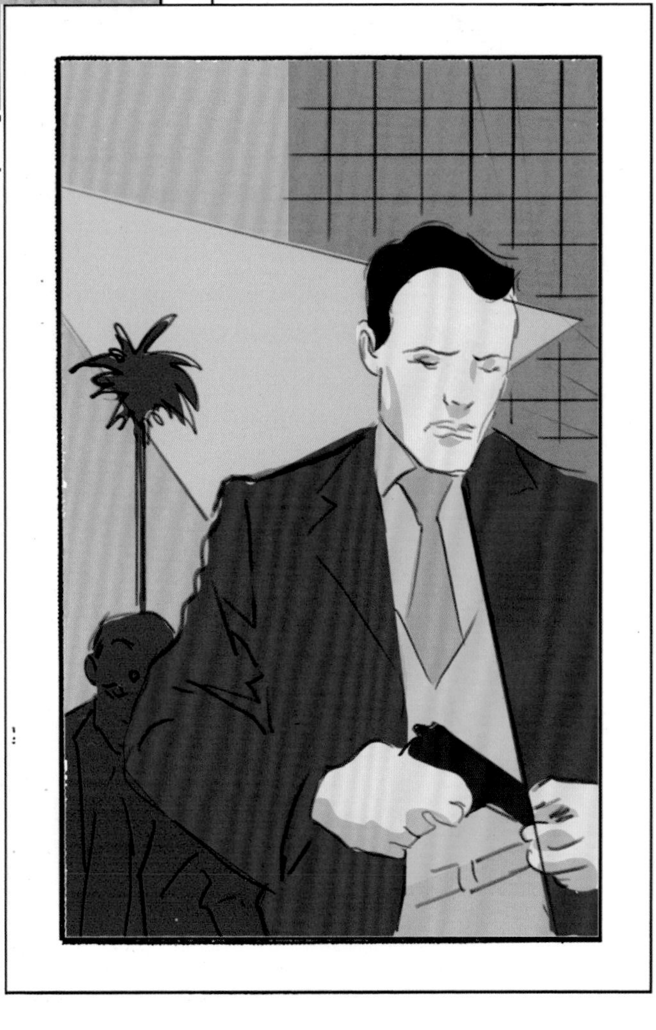

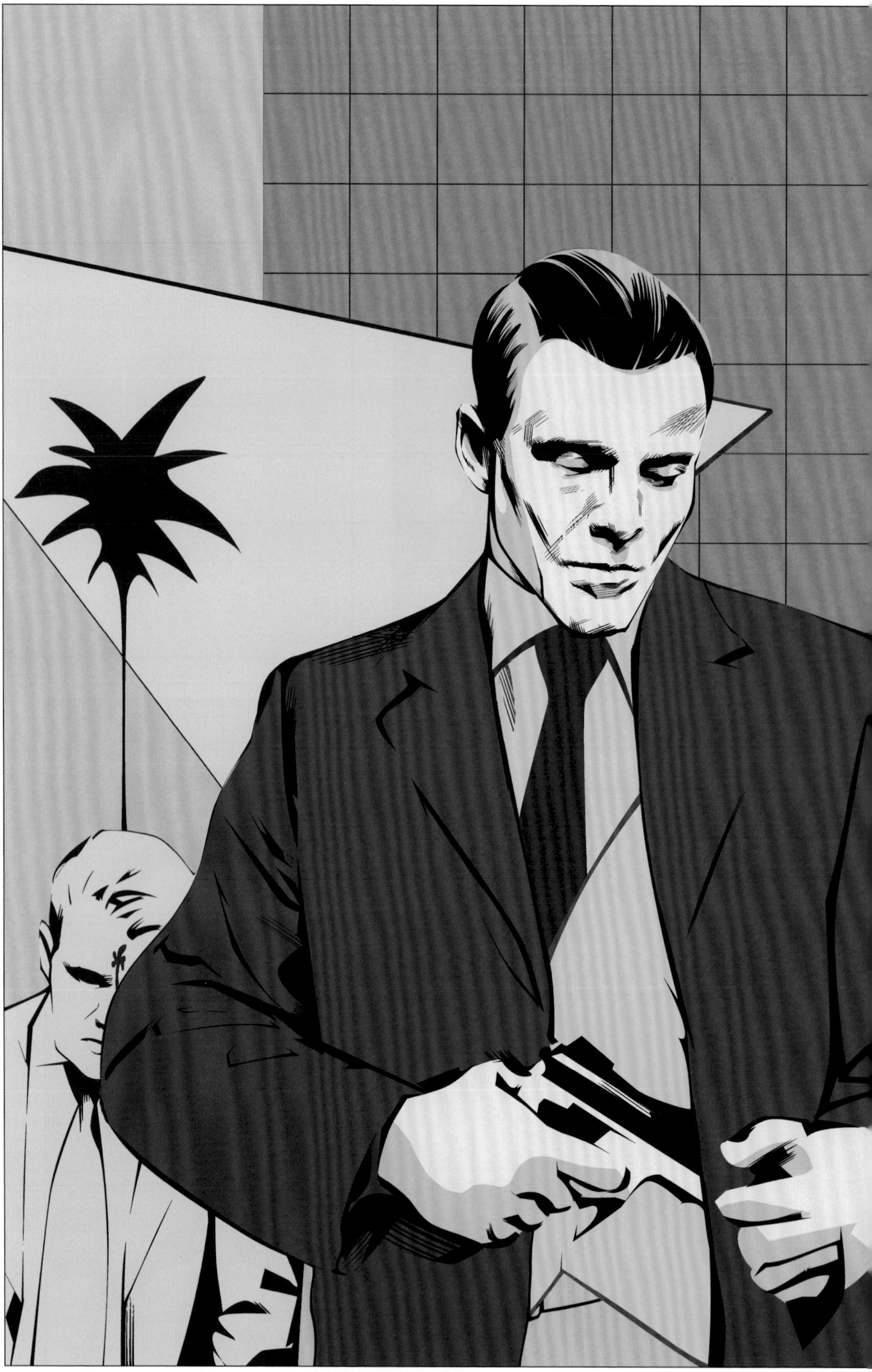

# SCRIPT SAMPLES by Dennis Calero

**The SUIT**

by Dennis Calero
Script for 20 Pages

PAGE 1

Entire page is framed by a 1980s/Will Eisner style designed panel border in the shape of the title of the Story: "Day at the Office" or, alternatively "Just Another Day at the Office," depending on what feels right.

This is a multi-tiered page with many small initial panels. The entire structure is meant to invoke Frank Miller and Chaykin of the early 80s, who, in turn, were trying to invoke Will Eisner of the 1950s.

(Rica, most of these are meant to be very small panels to establish a rhythm. If it seems like too much in the layouts, I can cut.)

Panel 1: Close up a closed pair of eyes, our main character, The Suit, asleep. His eyes are closed...but troubled.

Panel 2: An appropriately archaic alarm clock of the flip dial variety, it is 6:59 and we anticipate an alarm buzzing but...

Panel 3: The eyes are opened. Our "hero" is awake already.

Panel 4: Back to the clock, which is still on 6:59.

Panel 5: The clock, now it's 7:00 AM.

RADIO VOICE (vo)
...'s seven AM on this first day back to work in the year of our Lord, 1982, this is WBLS New York. I'm Murray the K...

Panel 6: The Suit rises. He is trim, strong. Michael Fassbender. Who should be everybody. Outside, the trees are bare but there's no snow. It's January 4th, the first Monday of 1982.

RADIO VOICE (vo)
National Security Adviser Richard Allen has resigned, to be replaced by Deputy Secretary of State Richard Clarke. The White House had no further comment. President Reagan returned yesterday from his home in Palm Springs, California.

Panel 7: He's down on the ground, in push up position.

RADIO VOICE (vo)
And actor Victor Buano of *Whatever Happened to Baby Jane* died over the weekend of a heart attack.

PAGE 1 (cont.)

Panel 8: He's lowered, blocked by the bed.

RADIO VOICE (vo)
He was forty three.

Panel 9: He's up again...

RADIO VOICE (vo)
It's twenty-six degrees in Central Park with snow expected later today.

Panel 10-12

Quick staccato panels, The Suit getting showered, dressed, shoes.

Panel 13:

Going downstairs, the family, a young buy, a younger girl, are sitting at the breakfast table, eating. The attractive wife is behind the counter. The TV blares in the bg.

The Suit is impeccably dressed in a power suit, his hair slicked back Gordon Gecko style, carrying a briefcase.

HOST (vo)
I'd like to welcome our new co-host, Bryant Gumble.

BRYANT GUMBLE (vo)
Thank you.

GIRL
Is it your birthday yet, Daddy?

SUIT
Not yet. Later this week.

BOY
How old *are* you, Daddy?

PAGE 1 (cont.)

Panel 14:

As he speaks, the girl is wrinkling her nose.

SUIT
I'll be forty-three.

GIRL
That's so *old,* daddy!

Panel 15: At the door...

He kisses his wife, but the gesture is somehow without warmth. Not hostile, but without feeling of any kind.

PAGE 2

Panel 1: He's exiting his idyllic house, his wife waving him on.

WIFE
Have a good day at work.

SUIT
I'll see you tonight.

Panel 2: He enters the sidewalk, falling into step with a number of neighbors, also suited and brief-cased...

Panel 3: Up the stairs to the Tarrytown train station, he spots a pal. Jerry is a little plump, gregarious. He worships the Suit, which is clear on his face.

JERRY
Good morning!

SUIT
Good morning, Jerry. Cold enough for you?

JERRY
Colder than a witch's tit. Eh, sorry, I know you don't like language.

SUIT
Never mind. They say it's going to snow.

Panel 4: They board the train. The Suit is giving Jerry a look.

JERRY
"Snow insulation isolates me from feeling
Cold sensation freezes me from all touch
The contrasting black emptiness inside."

SUIT
What?

JERRY
Ian Beckett. It's a poem.

Panel 5: The train heads along the Hudson River towards a distant Manhattan.

Writing for yourself is always dangerous, as your instinct is to kick the heavy lifting down the line. That's when artist-me curses writer-me for not working out some of the visual storytelling early on. Writing for others has made me do more of work on that end, leaving room for the artist to do his or her own thing.

PAGE 3:

Panel 1: Grand Central Station, main floor, The Suit and Jerry wave a casual good bye.

Panel 2: City street, cold breath emanating from the crowd of 1980s NY.

Panel 3: The Suit enters a modern office lobby, past the impossibly beautiful but disaffected secretaries...

Panel 4: ...exits an elevator onto a busy office floor...hands his briefcase, en route, to an assistant and...

Panel 5: ...enters a massive conference room overlooking a breathtaking view of Manhattan.  Around a modernist table of glass and steel sit three people, two old men, one man in his twenties evocative of Harrison Ford in "The Conversation."  The young man looks troubled, looking at the view.

> OLD MAN 1
> We've already started.

> SUIT
> Of course, sir.

---

PAGE 4

Panel 1: The Suit sits.  Old man 1 yells at the younger man, who is startled out of his reverie.  Old man 2 is sliding a newspaper over to the Suit's side of the table.

> OLD MAN 1
> Reginald, stop gawking out that window and pour
> the man a coffee!

> REGINALD
> Yes, father!

> OLD MAN 2
> To business.

Panel 2: Reginald pours coffee, while the Suit looks at a newspaper photo of a stern looking Japanese businessman.  Old Man 1 slams his fist onto the table.

> OLD MAN 2
> Yakatora is in town for one thing.

> OLD MAN 1
> He plans a hostile takeover of this company.  Our company!

> THE SUIT
> Thank you, Reginald.

> REGINALD
> You're welcome, sir.

Panel 3: The old men look stern, perhaps a bit crazed, like a real life version of Statler and Waldorf from the Muppets.

> OLD MAN 1
> This is unacceptable.

> OLD MAN 2
> Our offer of a merger has been denied.

> OLD MAN 1
> That yellow bastard.

> OLD MAN 2
> Now now, there's no call for that.

---

PAGE 5 :

Panel 1: On the Suit.

> OLD MAN 1
> My apologies, gentlemen.  The war.

> THE SUIT
> Of course, sir.

> OLD MAN 2
> We believe a face to face is necessary to resolve this conflict.

Panel 2: The Suit is rising.  In the bg, Reginald is staring out the window again, looking miserable.

> THE SUIT
> I have a lunch appointment with Mr. Yakamoto.  I will
> explain our position.

> OLD MAN 2
> Excellent.  On to new business?

Panel 3: The suit exits the conference room.  In the bg, Old man 1 is yelling at Reginald again.

> OLD MAN 1
> Stop staring out that window, boy, or by God I'll
> throw you out of it!

Panel 4: His assistant approaches with the briefcase.

> ASSISTANT
> Being tough on poor Reggie, aren't they?  Office
> romance gone bad, I hear.

> THE SUIT
> I don't like office gossip.

Panel 5: He's heading toward the elevator.

> ASSISTANT
> Sorry sir.  Will you be needing your briefcase?

> THE SUIT
> No.  This will be a brief meeting.

---

PAGE 5 (cont.)

Panel 6: The elevator door is closing between them.

> ASSISTANT
> Should I call you a taxi?

> THE SUIT
> I'll walk.

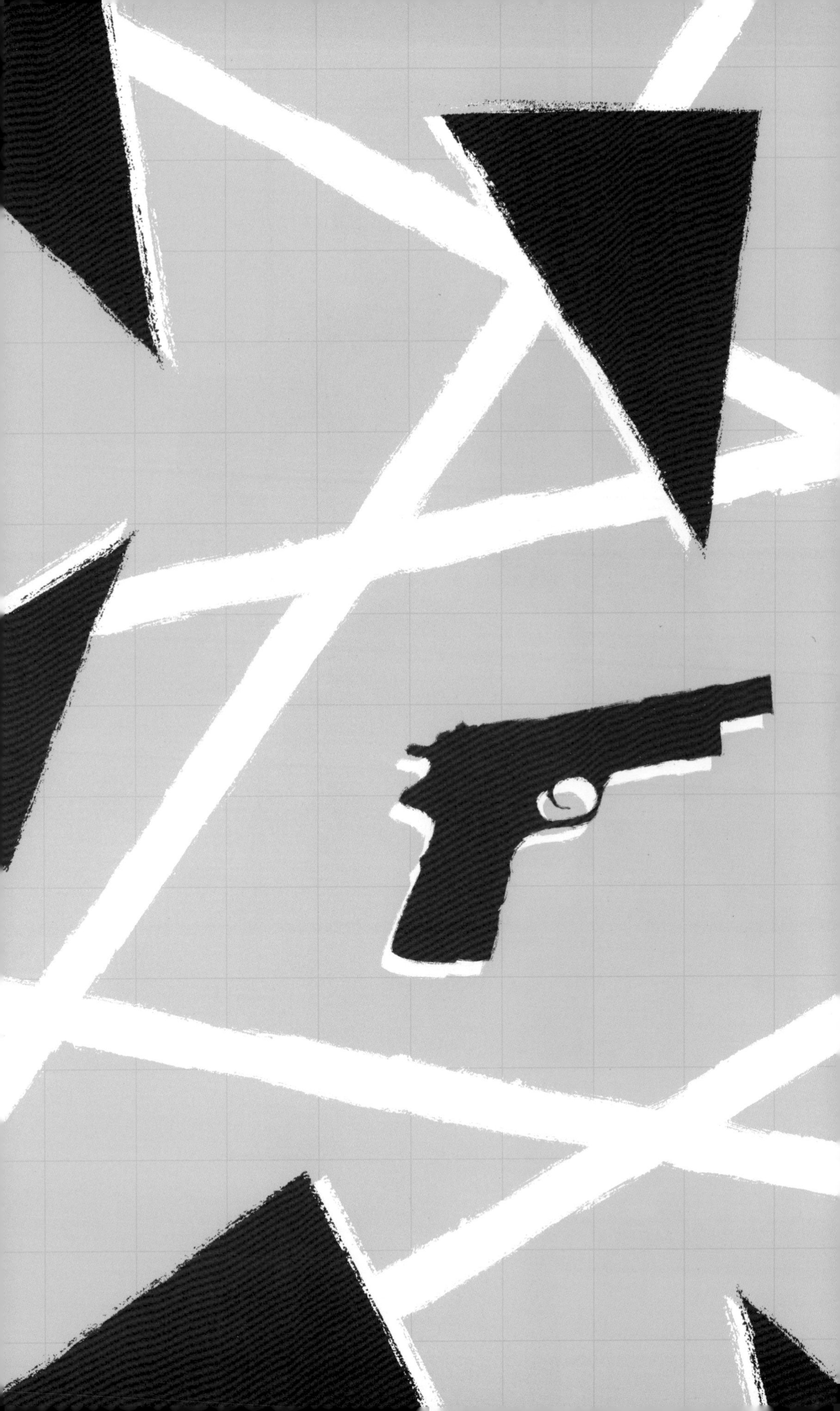

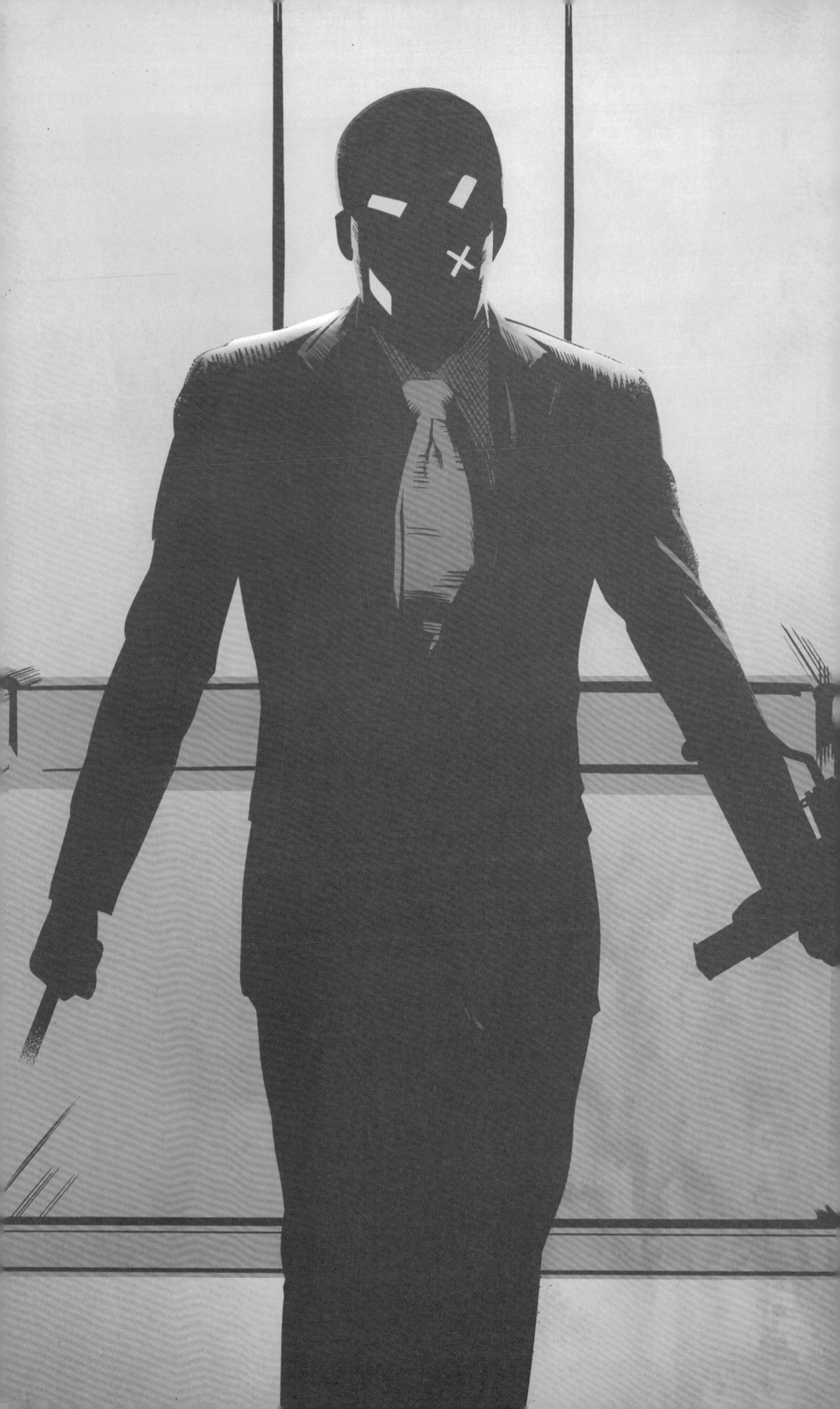